Inhaltsverzeichnis

Warming up

1 Vocabulary: How many words can you write with the letters of TRAVELLING?

____

____

Exercises

2 Irregular verbs: Write down the past forms of the verbs or drawings.

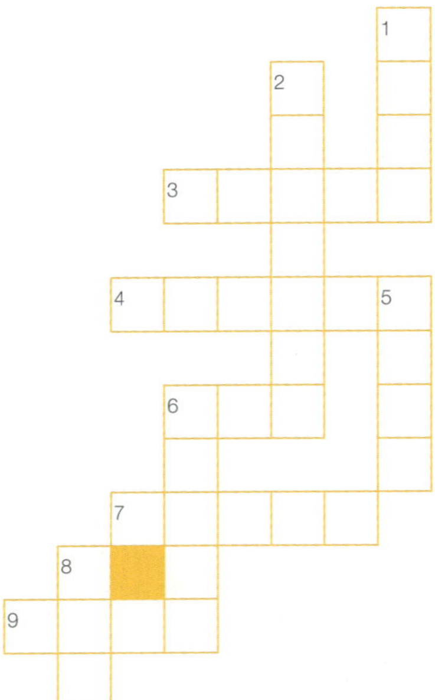

Across:
4. catch
7. find
9. make

Down:
2. bring
5. tell
8. see

3 Present or past simple: Fill in the correct form of the verbs in brackets. Then listen and check.

Key: 797

Key: 606

Interviewer: Why ______________ (you/like) travelling?
Samantha: It __________ (be) always exciting and a lot of fun.
You ____________ (see) different places and you ____________ (meet) different people.
Interviewer: Where ______________________ (you/usually/travel)?
Samantha: We often ______________ (go) to Italy or Croatia in summer.
Or we ______________ (visit) a European city like Paris, Rome or London.
Interviewer: ______________________ (you/take) a city break last year?
Samantha: No, last year we didn't. We ______________ (fly) to Australia in July.
That ______________ (be) great!
Interviewer: Wow! How long ______________________ (you/stay) there?
Samantha: For a month. We ______________ (spend) one week in Sydney and one in Melbourne.
Then we ______________ (take) the bus to Central Australia to see Ayers Rock. And after that we ______________ (go) snorkelling at the Great Barrier Reef.
It ______________ (be) fantastic!
Interviewer: That ______________ (sound) great.

4 Some – any: Fill in the correct form (some, any, something, anything, somebody, anybody, somewhere, anywhere). Then listen to check your answers.

Key: 352

Key: 190

This is what you need if you want to go camping: a tent, a table, ________________ chairs, ________________ to eat and drink and ________________ games for the children. There are also rules campers have to keep in mind: don't take __________ jewellery or ______________ expensive with you. Don't go ________________ isolated, stay at campsites. Never keep __________ food inside your tent because it might attract animals. Take _______________ friends with you if you like but don't ask ________________ you don't really get on well with*. Observe quiet hours and speed limits at the campsite. Don't give ________________ _______________ reason to be angry with you.

*sich mit jemandem gut verstehen

5 Vocabulary: Put the words from the box into the correct category.

French • sightseeing • Switzerland • travel guide • Spain • taking pictures • Czech • suitcase • Greek • visiting museums • Portuguese • passport • Great Britain • camera • Sweden • shopping

countries	nationalities	things you do when you travel	things you take with you when you travel

6 Present and past simple: Match the questions and the answers.

1. Where did you travel last summer?
2. Does your brother like taking the plane?
3. Where is my passport? I can't find it anywhere!
4. Why didn't he buy any souvenirs in Rome?

a. Check all your pockets again.
b. We didn't go anywhere because my mother was ill.
c. No, he doesn't. He prefers the train.
d. Because he didn't have any money left.

7 Writing: Create a travel blog about a holiday adventure.

Write about
- where you went
- how you got there
- what happened

Brain teaser

8 Vocabulary: Guess the words.

1. ehoweemsr ________________________
2. rusoeutPge ________________________
3. psarpost ________________________
4. hagcut ________________________

Warming up

1 Vocabulary: Match the pictures and the words.

glasses • curly hair • tall • sad • straight hair • beard •
tattoo • friendly • slim • freckles • bored • necklace

1. ______________

2. ______________

3. ______________

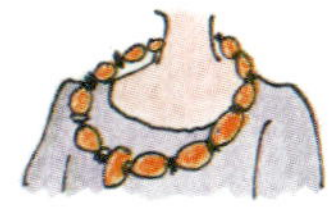
4. ______________

5. ______________

6. ______________

7. ______________

8. ______________

9. ______________

10. ______________

11. ______________

12. ______________

Exercises

2 Past continuous: Complete the sentences with the verbs from the box in the past continuous. Then listen and check.

Key: 901 Key: 506

shout • wear • (also) wear • drink • wave • smoke • sit

When I saw Kevin last week, I couldn't believe my eyes. He ______________ in a bar with two young men. They ______________ whisky and ______________ cigars. Kevin ______________ an old grey shirt and shabby jeans. He ______________ a strange hat. He ______________ his arms and ______________ four-letter words* at passers-by.

*Schimpfwörter

3 Relative pronouns: Complete the text with who, which, that or whose. Then listen to check your answers.

Key: 320 Key: 730

"Twilight" is a dark fantasy novel ______________ was written by Stephenie Meyer. It is the story of Bella Swan, a seventeen-year-old girl ______________ mother remarries. This is why Bella moves from Phoenix, Arizona, to Forks, Washington, to live with her father. There she meets Edward Cullen, ______________ is an attractive and mysterious boy. He saves her life at the school parking lot when he stops a van ______________ nearly knocks her down. After a while Edward and Bella fall in love. The girl finds out that Edward and his family are vampires ______________ all drink animal blood. If you want to know how the story continues, you have to read the book. Actually, "The Twilight Saga" is a series ______________ consists of four novels: Twilight, New Moon, Eclipse and Breaking Dawn. If you belong to those people ______________ prefer watching films, there are also five films ______________ you can watch.

4 Past continuous: What were these people doing yesterday at 4 p.m.? Look at the picture and write sentences.

____

____

____

5 Odd one out: Circle the word that doesn't belong in each line.

1. who which this that
2. blond dark grey blue
3. smile polite friendly nice
4. curly wavey straight hair
5. small tall slim bored

6 Writing: Choose one or two of the people from exercise 4 and write a story about them.

In your story
- describe the people (looks, clothes)
- explain what happened
- say how the story ended

Brain teaser

7 Past simple or continuous: Complete the sentences with the verbs in the correct tense. Then match them with the pictures.

a. 

b. 

c. 

d. 

1. While Celine ____________________ a book, her mobile ____________________.

2. When George ____________________ Helen at the cafe, she ____________________ a striped dress and big earrings.

3. First Michael ____________________ his homework, then he ____________________ to the cinema with Paul and Tom.

4. While Sandra ____________________ she ____________________ to her iPod.

Warming up

1 Vocabulary: Look at the pictures and fill in the missing letters.

1. a _ t _ r

2. _ c _ _ _ ce f _ _ ti _ n f _ _ m

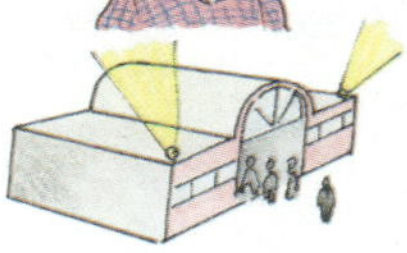
3. _ i _ e _ a

4. f _ _ m d _ r _ ct _ _

5. _ dv _ _ t _ re _ il _

6. sp _ _ _ al _ ff _ ct _

Exercises

2 Comparison of adjectives: Look at the information about the three films and tick the sentences true (T) or false (F). Then listen and check.

Key: 990 Key: 723

Forever
Year: 2014
Oscars: 2
Budget: $ 50,000,000
Duration: 92 minutes

Scary Island
Year: 2015
Oscars: 1
Budget: $ 80,000,000
Duration: 118 minutes

James Blond
Year: 2013
Oscars: 0
Budget: $ 100,000,000
Duration: 122 minutes

	T	F
1. *Scary Island* is older than *Forever*.		
2. *Forever* won more Oscars than *James Blond* but fewer than *Scary Island*.		
3. *James Blond* is the oldest film.		
4. *Forever* cost less than *Scary Island* but more than *James Blond*.		
5. *Scary Island* is shorter than *James Blond* but longer than *Forever*.		
6. *Forever* won as many Oscars as *Scary Island*.		
7. The most expensive film is *James Blond*.		
8. *Scary Island* is not as old as *James Blond*.		
9. *Scary Island* is not the shortest film.		

3 Comparison of adjectives: Complete the sentences with the correct form of the adjectives.

This is what people say about films:

1. The first part of the film was ______________________ (exciting) than the second.
2. This film lasts ______________________ (long) than the film we saw last week.
3. This is ______________________ (bad) movie I've ever seen.
4. Watching a film on DVD is ______________________ (not fascinating) as watching it at the cinema.
5. Comedies are ______________________ (funny) than romantic films.

4 Modal verb *allowed to*: Complete the sentences with the correct form of allowed to. Then match them with the pictures. Mind the tenses!

Key: 265

a. ☐ 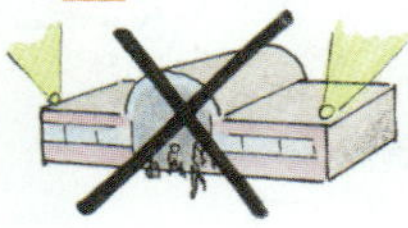

b. ☐ 

c. ☐ 

d. ☐ 

e. ☐ 

1. You ______________________________
2. Ann and Mark ______________________________
3. I ______________________________ yesterday because I had to finish my homework.
4. ______________________________ when you were young?
5. Next Saturday we ______________________________ all night long.

5 Writing: Write a film review about your favourite film. Write about

- the plot
- the main characters
- why you like the film

Brain teaser

6 Reading comprehension and modal verbs can/be able to: Fill in the correct form of can or be able to (- - - - - - - -) and complete the dialogues with the sentences from below (________). Listen to check your answers.

Key: 851 Key: 262

Peter: ______________________________

Megan: I'm afraid I - - - - - - - - - - - - go to the cinema with you tonight. I have to study for my maths test.

Peter: ______________________________

Megan: I know. I would love to see "Pepper". ______________ you tell me tomorrow what it is about?

Peter: I'm sorry. I - - - - - - - - - - - - (never) remember the plot of a film.

Megan: ______________________________

Peter: Because I admire Angelina Jolie. She - - - - - - - - - - - - do most of her stunts herself.

Megan: ______________________________ A couple of weeks ago her film "Maleficent" was on TV. Unfortunately I - - - - - - - - - - - - watch it because my little sister was crying all night so that I didn't understand a word.

Peter: Never mind. I have it on DVD, so we - - - - - - - - - - - - watch it at my place whenever you want.

Megan: ______________________________

That's a pity! • Great, thanks. • That's amazing. • can • What's the matter, Megan? • Why are you going to the cinema then?

1 Riddle: Complete the sentences with the words from the pictures.

1. When you travel, you usually take a lot of ____________________.
2. A brilliant actor or actress maybe wins an ____________________.
3. People who have curly hair often prefer ____________________ hair.
4. In his dreams he often flies into ____________________ and walks on the moon.
5. Pippi Longstocking* has got lots of ____________________ in her face.
6. If I won the ____________________, I would buy a fast car.
7. Most people have got a computer but not all of them have got a ____________________.
8. Last night Ben had a strange dream. He ____________________ Britney Spears!

*Pippi Langstrumpf

Then take the following letters of the words you filled in to find out the author's favourite films: from 2 the 4th letter, from 1 the 3rd letter, from 3 the 2nd and the 5th letter, from 6 the 2nd letter, from 7 the 4th letter, from 5 the 1st letter, from 7 the 3rd letter, from 6 the 1st letter, from 8 the 1st letter, and from 4 the 1st letter.

The author's favourite films are _ _ _ _ _ _ _   _ _ _ _ _ _

2 Tongue twisters*: Try to say the following tongue twisters aloud. How fast can you say them?

*Zungenbrecher

I scream, you scream, we all scream for ice cream!

She sells sea shells by the sea shore

Red lorry, yellow lorry

Whether the weather is warm, whether the weather is hot, we have to put up with the weather, whether we like it or not.

A big black bug bit a big black dog on his big black nose.

Betty Botter bought a bit of butter. "But," she said, "this butter's bitter! If I put it in my batter, it will make my batter bitter!" So she bought a bit of butter better than her bitter butter, And she put it in her batter, and her batter was not bitter. So 'twas better Betty Botter bought a bit of better butter.

3 Riddles: Match the questions to the answers. Try to guess the answers first.

1. **During what month do people sleep the least?**
2. **What two things can you never eat for breakfast?**
3. *What can you catch but not throw?*
4. *What kind of room has no doors or windows?*
5. **What belongs to you but others use it more than you do?**
6. **What jumps higher than a building?**
7. *How many seconds are in a year?*
8. *I'm as light as a feather, yet the strongest man can't hold me for more than 5 minutes. What am I?*
9. **Timmy's mother has three children. The first was named April. The next was named May. What is the third child's name?**

A mushroom.

Lunch and dinner.

Breath

A cold.

Timmy.

Only 12. January 2nd, February 2nd, etc.

Your name.

Everything. A building can't jump.

February, it's the shortest month after all.

4 Look at the clues and find out the words about films.

Capital of Norway ~~3~~ ~~4~~ +  = ______________________

Capital of Italy ~~4~~ +  +  ~~3~~ = ______________________ film

↓  ~~4~~ + ly +  = ______________________

Warming up

1 Vocabulary: Write down the words and phrases from the word snake.

2 Good luck or bad luck? Put the words and phrases into the categories below.

good luck	bad luck

Exercises

3 Superstitions/if-sentences type 1: Finish the sentences using the phrases in the box.

Key: 338 Key: 295

1. If you throw broken dishes at the houses of friends and family on New Year's Eve, __________
2. If you open and close scissors without cutting anything, __________
3. If you put your bread upside-down on the table, __________
4. If you let your wallet or purse hit the floor, __________
5. If you eat 12 grapes one after another when the clock strikes 12 on New Year's Eve, __________
6. If you go to sleep with a fan* on in your room, __________
7. If bird droppings** land on you, __________

*Ventilator **Kot

you will be hungry. • it will kill you. • they will have good luck in the New Year. • you will be rich. • you will lose money. • you will have bad luck. • you will have good luck for twelve months.

Now match the superstitions with the countries where they come from. Guess! Then listen and check your answers.

France: ______ Russia: ______ Denmark: ______ South Korea: ______
Spain: ______ Egypt: ______ Brazil: ______

4 Modal verbs must/have to: Rewrite the sentence "Andrea wears something blue at her wedding." using the correct forms of must or have to.

Key: 473

Present tense	1. Ann ______ 2. ______
Past tense	______
Present Perfect Tense	______
Will-future	______

5 If-sentences type 1: Complete the sentences.

1. If it ______ (rain) tomorrow, they will stay at home.
2. I will have good luck if ______.
3. If people throw rice at a wedding, the couple ______ (have) many children.
4. ______ if she knocks on wood.
5. If we have time, ______.

6 Writing: Write a text about the rules in your house. Write about

- what you have to do
- what you don't have to do
- what you mustn't do (= aren't allowed to do)

Brain teaser

Key: 707

7 Listening comprehension: Listen to Peter's story about his terrible day and tick the correct answers.

1. Peter's alarm clock didn't ring
   - ☐ last Thursday.
   - ☐ last Friday.
   - ☐ last Tuesday.
2. When the boy prepared breakfast,
   - ☐ his mum broke a cup.
   - ☐ his mum cleaned up the mess.
   - ☐ his mum smashed an egg.
3. Before Peter went to the bus stop, he was looking for his
   - ☐ school bag.
   - ☐ test book.
   - ☐ lucky stone.
4. He arrived at school
   - ☐ 20 minute late.
   - ☐ 30 minutes late.
   - ☐ 40 minutes late.
5. After school the boy had to walk home because
   - ☐ he had missed the bus.
   - ☐ it was raining.
   - ☐ the bus had broken down.
6. He got home
   - ☐ totally wet.
   - ☐ very dirty.
   - ☐ dry.
7. The fridge was all empty because
   - ☐ nobody had done the shopping.
   - ☐ his sister's classmates had been there.
   - ☐ his sister had eaten up everything.

Warming up

1 Vocabulary: Think of things you dream about and write a word with each letter. Then do the same with "dilemma" but here the letters can also be in the middle of the words

D ______________
R ______________
E ______________
A ______________
M ______________
S ______________

__________D__________
__________I__________
__________L__________
__________E__________
__________M__________
__________M__________
__________A__________

Exercises

2 Past participles: Put the word halves together to find out the past participles. Then write them down.

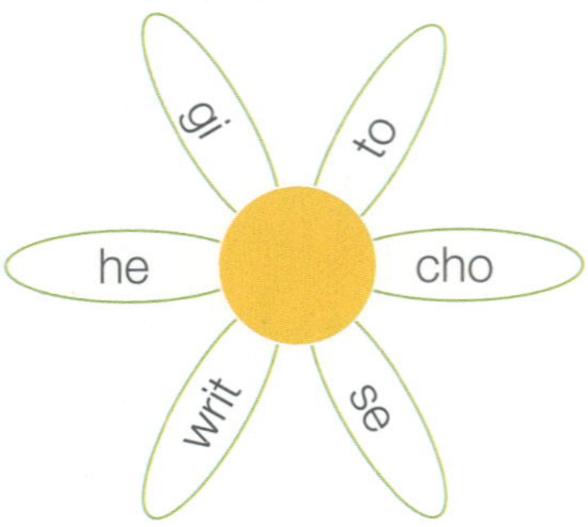

____
____
____
____
____
____

3 Past perfect tense: Fill in the past perfect forms of the verbs in brackets. Here are some sentences about dreams people had.

Key: 298

1. Kate's dream: After she ______________ (meet) Tom Cruise, they got married and had three children.
2. Eve's dream: She worked as a model because she ______________ (take part) in a talent show.
3. Ethan's dream: Before the police arrived, he ______________ (rob) the bank and ______________ (escape).
4. Luke's dream: He landed on the moon and took a walk there after he ______________ (fly) into space.
5. Jenny's dream: She travelled around the world because she ______________ (win) the lottery.

4 If-sentences – type 2: Choose a), b) or c) to finish the sentences.

Key: 802

1. If I	a. remembered	b. remember	c. would remember	my dream, I would tell it to you.
2. What	a. did	b. do	c. would	you do if you found a bag full of money?
3. Laura	a. were	b. was	c. would be	very happy if Peter left his girlfriend.
4. If they	a. would meet	b. met	c. meet	a famous pop star, they wouldn't know what to say.

5 Past perfect tense: Matt's dream – Look at the pictures and complete the sentences with the verbs in past or past perfect tense.

Key: 507

Last night Matt ______________ (have) an exciting dream. After he ________________ (miss) the train, he ______________ (follow) it in a hot air balloon and ______________ (fly) on a snow-covered mountain. On top of the mountain Matt ______________ (put) on his skis. After he ______________ (go) downhill, he ______________ (jump) on a ship. He ________________ (get off) the ship, before he ______________ (take) a motorbike. As fast as he ______________ (can), he ______________ (go) to the station where the train he ______________ (miss) was waiting. In the morning Matt's mother ____________________ (wake him up) and he __________ (feel) sad because it ____________________ (only be) a dream.

6 Writing: Write the answer that the agony aunt* wrote to Vanessa. In your letter

- tell Vanessa what you think about her problem
- give her some advice what she should do
- tell her what she shouldn't do

Brain teaser

7 Reading comprehension: The following problem letter that Vanessa wrote to an agony aunt* is in jumbled order. Put it into the correct order, then listen and check.

*Kummerkastentante

Key: 694

- ☐ They also make fun of my clothes and my hairstyle, but they only do it when the teacher isn't around.
- ☐ Vanessa
- ☐ They are always very busy and have enough problems themselves.
- 1 **Dear Agony aunt,**
- ☐ The other classmates don't seem to like me either. So I never speak to anyone.
- ☐ At my new school there are two boys who keep calling me names and the others love every time they do it.
- ☐ I feel really depressed and I don't want to go to school anymore. What should I do? Please help me.
- ☐ I'm a 13-year-old girl and I'm having a lot of problems at the moment. I don't know who to turn to for help.
- ☐ Six months ago we moved to a new town and my parents started new jobs.

1 Wordsearch: Find 16 words about travelling, stories, films and superstitions (four words each).

T	R	O	P	S	S	A	P	C	A	G	V	M	S	I
E	G	S	Y	M	O	P	A	F	K	N	P	I	O	C
U	S	Y	O	O	Y	M	E	L	N	I	R	R	U	A
Z	S	N	T	K	P	S	J	I	A	D	R	R	V	E
P	B	T	J	S	R	O	T	C	A	D	O	O	E	X
X	A	Z	I	V	I	M	D	E	U	E	D	R	N	V
T	E	T	R	P	V	U	I	I	R	W	A	E	I	C
P	E	S	N	O	R	K	E	L	L	I	N	G	R	F
U	U	W	R	W	T	F	R	I	S	C	O	D	S	C
S	C	R	E	A	M	C	H	I	U	Z	V	U	O	D
N	L	F	A	N	R	A	E	R	L	D	X	U	S	B
O	H	T	X	U	L	E	L	R	N	T	K	N	E	Z
J	W	S	W	I	P	Y	G	P	I	O	C	U	F	F
H	W	H	I	E	A	P	E	O	G	D	U	D	I	F
F	P	D	H	R	L	X	G	E	C	Y	L	M	Q	L

Travelling: ______________________________

____

Stories: ______________________________

____

Films: ______________________________

____

Superstitions: ______________________________

____

2 Word order: Put the words in the correct order.

1. cinema | is | of | who | girl | is | in | the | cousin | front | The | my | waiting

____

2. wasn't | some | wanted | any | there | eat | cream | We | to | but | left | ice

____

3. than | your | interesting | book | mine? | Was | more

____

4. her | play | with | had | went | to | her | After | exercises, | she | out | she | friends | finished

____

3 If sentences 1 and 2: Match the sentence halves.

1. If he loved her, he
2. If I was a teacher, I
3. If you go to England, you
4. If they took the plane, they
5. If she doesn't help her dad, he
6. If we don't hurry up, we

a. will be very angry.
b. would have to pay more.
c. will have to speak English.
d. won't be there in time.
e. would buy her a diamond ring.
f. wouldn't give any homework.

4 Mixed tenses: Fill in present simple or continuous, past simple or continuous or past perfect tense. Then listen and check.

Key: 535

Sally: Hello?
Harry: Hi, Sally, this ____________ (be) Harry. What ____________ (you/do)?
Sally: ____________ (I/watch) Harry Potter.
Harry: ____________ (you/not watch) it when I ____________ (call) you yesterday?
Sally: Yes, that ____________ (be) true. I ____________ (love) Harry Potter. I ____________ (watch) it every day. And what ____________ (you/do)?
Harry: Nothing. After I ____________ (phone) you yesterday, I ____________ (want) to rent a Harry Potter DVD but I ____________ (cannot get) one. ____________ (can) I come over to your place to watch the film with you?
Sally: Sure, no problem. Bring along some crisps.

5 Modal verbs: Your English teacher is asking a lot of questions. Fill in the correct form and answer the questions so that they are true for you. Use present or past tense.

1. ____________ you ski? ____________ (can)
2. ____________ go to bed early when you were eight years old? (must) ____________
3. ____________ eat lots of sweets? (you/allowed to) ____________
4. ____________ help your mother with the housework? (must) ____________
5. ____________ speak English when you were three years old? (can) ____________

6 Dilemmas and dreams: Finish the sentences to express what you would do.

Dilemmas:
If I broke my friend's favourite CD or DVD, ____________
If my dog ate my English homework, ____________
My father would be very angry if ____________

Dreams:
One of my biggest dreams would come true if ____________
____
If I were a millionaire, ____________
If I met the boy / girl of my dreams, ____________

7 If-sentences 1 and 2: Put the verbs in brackets into the correct form.

A: Joe, what ____________ (do) if you ____________ (be) rich?
B: Let me think. I ____________ (buy) a Ferrari, a helicopter and a nice house.
A: And ____________ (give) part of the money to your friends too if you ____________ (have) enough of it?
B: No, I ____________ (not do) so even if I ____________ (be) a millionaire.
A: If you ____________ (not be nice) to your friends, you ____________ (lose) them.
B: I don't need friends who are only interested in my money.

Warming up

1 London sights: Match the pictures and the words.

Tower Bridge • London Eye • Buckingham Palace • Big Ben • Trafalgar Square • St. Paul's Cathedral

ingimage.com

1. ______________________

VERITAS-VERLAG, Linz/Susanne Suk

2. ______________________

ingimage.com

3. ______________________

ingimage.com

3. ______________________

ingimage.com

5. ______________________

VERITAS-VERLAG, Linz/Susanne Suk

6. ______________________

Exercises

2 Present perfect tense domino: Write down the past participles that are hidden in the four domino snakes. The last letter of a word is also the first letter of the next one.

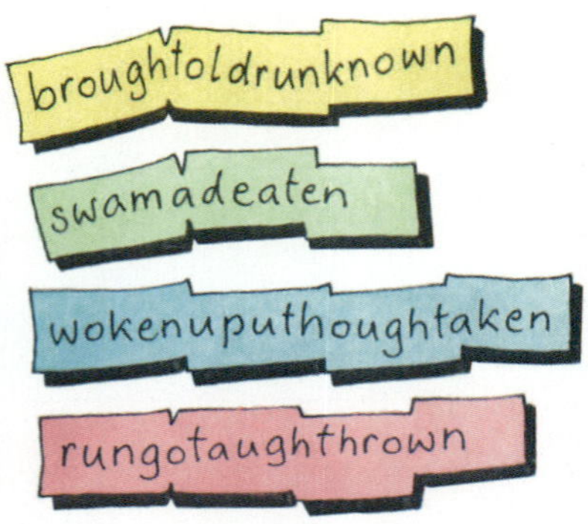

1. ______________________
2. ______________________
3. ______________________
4. ______________________

3 Present perfect tense – for or since? Circle the correct word.

Key: 906

1. My uncle has lived in Oxford Street for / since twenty years.
2. I haven't spoken German for / since I arrived in London.
3. Buckingham Palace has been the official residence of Britain's monarchs for / since 1837.
4. I have queued* for / since two hours to get tickets for the London Eye.
5. Janet hasn't seen her friends from London for / since last Christmas.
6. Big Ben has been one of the world's most famous tourist attractions for / since many years.

* sich anstellen

LÖSUNGEN

3

3. Klasse NMS/AHS

VERITAS
Gemeinsam besser lernen

Warming up

1 Vocabulary: How many words can you write with the letters of TRAVELLING?

train, ring, line, rave, ear, lie, veal, navel, get, girl, give, gave, nag, tell, tag, tin, till, ran, rag, art, great, gin, live, let, rail ...

Exercises

2 Irregular verbs: Write down the past forms of the verbs or drawings.

Across:
4. catch
7. find
9. make

Down:
2. bring
5. tell
8. see

3 Present or past simple: Fill in the correct form of the verbs in brackets. Then listen and check.

Key: 797

Key: 606

Interviewer: Why do you like (you/like) travelling?
Samantha: It is (be) always exciting and a lot of fun. You see (see) different places and you meet (meet) different people.
Interviewer: Where do you usually travel (you/usually/travel)?
Samantha: We often go (go) to Italy or Croatia in summer. Or we visit (visit) a European city like Paris, Rome or London.
Interviewer: Did you take (you/take) a city break last year?
Samantha: No, last year we didn't. We flew (fly) to Australia in July. That was (be) great!
Interviewer: Wow! How long did you stay (you/stay) there?
Samantha: For a month. We spent (spend) one week in Sydney and one in Melbourne. Then we took (take) the bus to Central Australia to see Ayers Rock. And after that we went (go) snorkelling at the Great Barrier Reef. It was (be) fantastic!
Interviewer: That sounds (sound) great.

4 Some – any: Fill in the correct form (some, any, something, anything, somebody, anybody, somewhere, anywhere). Then listen to check your answers.

Key: 352

Key: 190

This is what you need if you want to go camping: a tent, a table, some chairs, something to eat and drink and some games for the children. There are also rules campers have to keep in mind: don't take any jewellery or anything expensive with you. Don't go anywhere isolated, stay at campsites. Never keep any food inside your tent because it might attract animals. Take some friends with you if you like but don't ask anybody you don't really get on well with*. Observe quiet hours and speed limits at the campsite. Don't give anybody any reason to be angry with you.

*sich mit jemandem gut verstehen

5 Vocabulary: Put the words from the box into the correct category.

French • sightseeing • Switzerland • travel guide • Spain • taking pictures • Czech • suitcase • Greek • visiting museums • Portuguese • passport • Great Britain • camera • Sweden • shopping

countries	nationalities	things you do when you travel	things you take with you when you travel
Switzerland	French	sightseeing	travel guide
Spain	Czech	taking pictures	suitcase
Great Britain	Greek	visiting museums	passport
Sweden	Portuguese	shopping	camera

6 Present and past simple: Match the questions and the answers.

1. Where did you travel last summer?
2. Does your brother like taking the plane?
3. Where is my passport? I can't find it anywhere!
4. Why didn't he buy any souvenirs in Rome?

a. Check all your pockets again.
b. We didn't go anywhere because my mother was ill.
c. No, he doesn't. He prefers the train.
d. Because he didn't have any money left.

(1 – b, 2 – c, 3 – a, 4 – d)

7 Writing: Create a travel blog about a holiday adventure.

Write about
- where you went
- how you got there
- what happened

Example: Ireland – what a fascinating country! When we arrived at the airport of Dublin, the sun was shining, which is quite unusual as it normally rains every day in Ireland. You never guess what happened right after our arrival. We took the bus to the centre of Dublin and started our sightseeing tour when we suddenly bumped into Bono Vox from U2! He was really friendly although I was speechless. He even gave us an autograph! ...

Brain teaser

8 Vocabulary: Guess the words.

1. ehoweemsr somewhere
2. rusoeutPge Portuguese
3. psarpost passport
4. hagcut caught

Warming up

1 Vocabulary: Match the pictures and the words.

glasses • curly hair • tall • sad • straight hair • beard •
tattoo • friendly • slim • freckles • bored • necklace

1. beard

2. bored

3. straight hair

4. necklace

5. friendly

6. slim

7. freckles

8. curly hair

9. tattoo

10. sad

11. tall

12. glasses

Exercises

Key: 901 Key: 506

2 Past continuous: Complete the sentences with the verbs from the box in the past continuous. Then listen and check.

shout • wear • (also) wear • drink • wave • smoke • sit

When I saw Kevin last week, I couldn't believe my eyes. He was sitting in a bar with two young men. They were drinking whisky and smoking cigars. Kevin was wearing an old grey shirt and shabby jeans. He was (also) wearing a strange hat. He was waving his arms and shouting four-letter words* at passers-by.

*Schimpfwörter

Key: 320 Key: 730

3 Relative pronouns: Complete the text with who, which, that or whose. Then listen to check your answers.

"Twilight" is a dark fantasy novel which was written by Stephenie Meyer. It is the story of Bella Swan, a seventeen-year-old girl whose mother remarries. This is why Bella moves from Phoenix, Arizona, to Forks, Washington, to live with her father. There she meets Edward Cullen, who is an attractive and mysterious boy. He saves her life at the school parking lot when he stops a van that nearly knocks her down. After a while Edward and Bella fall in love. The girl finds out that Edward and his family are vampires who all drink animal blood. If you want to know how the story continues, you have to read the book. Actually, "The Twilight Saga" is a series which consists of four novels: Twilight, New Moon, Eclipse and Breaking Dawn. If you belong to those people who prefer watching films, there are also five films that you can watch.

4 Past continuous: What were these people doing yesterday at 4 p.m.? Look at the picture and write sentences.

An old man was sleeping on a sunbed. Two boys were playing football.
A girl was talking on the phone/telephoning.
A man and a woman were drinking coffee and a cat was chasing a mouse.

5 Odd one out: Circle the word that doesn't belong in each line.

1. who which (this) that
2. blond dark grey (blue)
3. (smile) polite friendly nice
4. curly wavey straight (hair)
5. small tall slim (bored)

6 Writing: Choose one or two of the people from exercise 4 and write a story about them.

In your story
- describe the people (looks, clothes)
- explain what happened
- say how the story ended

Brain teaser

7 Past simple or continuous: Complete the sentences with the verbs in the correct tense. Then match them with the pictures.

a. 
b. 

c. 
d. 

1. While Celine was reading a book, her mobile rang. c
2. When George met Helen at the cafe, she was wearing a striped dress and big earrings. d
3. First Michael did/finished his homework, then he went to the cinema with Paul and Tom. b
4. While Sandra was jogging/running she was listening to her iPod. a

Warming up

1 Vocabulary: Look at the pictures and fill in the missing letters.

1. actor
2. science fiction film
3. cinema
4. film director
5. adventure film
6. special effects

Exercises

2 Comparison of adjectives: Look at the information about the three films and tick the sentences true (T) or false (F). Then listen and check.

Key: 990 Key: 723

Forever
Year: 2014
Oscars: 2
Budget: $ 50,000,000
Duration: 92 minutes

Scary Island
Year: 2015
Oscars: 1
Budget: $ 80,000,000
Duration: 118 minutes

James Blond
Year: 2013
Oscars: 0
Budget: $ 100,000,000
Duration: 122 minutes

	T	F
1. *Scary Island* is older than *Forever*.		x
2. *Forever* won more Oscars than *James Blond* but fewer than *Scary Island*.		x
3. *James Blond* is the oldest film.	x	
4. *Forever* cost less than *Scary Island* but more than *James Blond*.		x
5. *Scary Island* is shorter than *James Blond* but longer than *Forever*.	x	
6. *Forever* won as many Oscars as *Scary Island*.		x
7. The most expensive film is *James Blond*.	x	
8. *Scary Island* is not as old as *James Blond*.	x	
9. *Scary Island* is not the shortest film.	x	

3 Comparison of adjectives: Complete the sentences with the correct form of the adjectives.

This is what people say about films:

1. The first part of the film was more exciting (exciting) than the second.
2. This film lasts longer (long) than the film we saw last week.
3. This is the worst (bad) movie I've ever seen.
4. Watching a film on DVD is not as fascinating (not fascinating) as watching it at the cinema.
5. Comedies are funnier (funny) than romantic films.

4 Modal verb *allowed to*: Complete the sentences with the correct form of allowed to. Then match them with the pictures. Mind the tenses!

Key: 265

a. 3 b. 5 c. 1 d. 2 e. 4

1. You are allowed to eat popcorn at the cinema.
2. Ann and Mark are not allowed to watch TV after ten pm.
3. I wasn't allowed to go to the cinema yesterday because I had to finish my homework.
4. Were you allowed to watch horror films when you were young?
5. Next Saturday we will be allowed / are allowed to watch DVDs all night long.

5 Writing: Write a film review about your favourite film. Write about

- the plot
- the main characters
- why you like the film

Example: One of the best films I've ever seen is The Florida Puzzle. The main characters are Brad Cruise and Penelope Diaz. The film is about a detective who is looking for his girlfriend and ...

Brain teaser

6 Reading comprehension and modal verbs can/be able to: Fill in the correct form of can or be able to ( ) and complete the dialogues with the sentences from below ( ). Listen to check your answers.

Key: 851 Key: 262

Peter: What's the matter, Megan?
Megan: I'm afraid I won't be able to / can't go to the cinema with you tonight. I have to study for my maths test.
Peter: That's a pity!
Megan: I know. I would love to see "Pepper". Can / Could you tell me tomorrow what it is about?
Peter: I'm sorry. I have never been able to (never) remember the plot of a film.
Megan: Why are you going to the cinema then?
Peter: Because I admire Angelina Jolie. She can / is able to do most of her stunts herself.
Megan: That's amazing. A couple of weeks ago her film "Maleficent" was on TV. Unfortunately I couldn't watch it because my little sister was crying all night so that I didn't understand a word.
Peter: Never mind. I have it on DVD, so we can watch it at my place whenever you want.
Megan: Great, thanks.

That's a pity! • Great, thanks. • That's amazing. • can • What's the matter, Megan? • Why are you going to the cinema then?

1 Riddle: Complete the sentences with the words from the pictures.

1. When you travel, you usually take a lot of pictures.
2. A brilliant actor or actress maybe wins an oscar.
3. People who have curly hair often prefer straight hair.
4. In his dreams he often flies into space and walks on the moon.
5. Pippi Longstocking* has got lots of freckles in her face.
6. If I won the lottery, I would buy a fast car.
7. Most people have got a computer but not all of them have got a printer.
8. Last night Ben had a strange dream. He married Britney Spears!

*Pippi Langstrumpf

Then take the following letters of the words you filled in to find out the author's favourite films: from 2 the 4th letter, from 1 the 3rd letter, from 3 the 2nd and the 5th letter, from 6 the 2nd letter, from 7 the 4th letter, from 5 the 1st letter, from 7 the 3rd letter, from 6 the 1st letter, from 8 the 1st letter, and from 4 the 1st letter.

The author's favourite films are a c t i o n f i l m s

2 Tongue twisters*: Try to say the following tongue twisters aloud. How fast can you say them?

*Zungenbrecher

I scream, you scream, we all scream for ice cream!

She sells sea shells by the sea shore

Red lorry, yellow lorry

A big black bug bit a big black dog on his big black nose.

Whether the weather is warm, whether the weather is hot, we have to put up with the weather, whether we like it or not.

Betty Botter bought a bit of butter. "But," she said, "this butter's bitter! If I put it in my batter, it will make my batter bitter!" So she bought a bit of butter better than her bitter butter, And she put it in her batter, and her batter was not bitter. So 'twas better Betty Botter bought a bit of better butter.

3 Riddles: Match the questions to the answers. Try to guess the answers first.

1. During what month do people sleep the least?
2. What two things can you never eat for breakfast?
3. *What can you catch but not throw?*
4. *What kind of room has no doors or windows?*
5. What belongs to you but others use it more than you do?
6. What jumps higher than a building?
7. *How many seconds are in a year?*
8. *I'm as light as a feather, yet the strongest man can't hold me for more than 5 minutes. What am I?*
9. Timmy's mother has three children. The first was named April. The next was named May. What is the third child's name?

February, it's the shortest month after all.

Everything. A building can't jump.

Your name.

Only 12. January 2nd, February 2nd, etc.

Timmy.

A cold.

Breath

Lunch and dinner.

A mushroom.

4 Look at the clues and find out the words about films.

Capital of Norway (-3 -4) +  = Oscar

Capital of Italy (-4) +  +  (-3) = romantic film

 (-4) + ly +  = Hollywood

Warming up

1 Vocabulary: Write down the words and phrases from the word snake.

walk under a ladder, four leaf clover, shooting star, break a mirror, black cat, hear a cuckoo, the number thirteen, tiger's eye, blow out all candles, cross your fingers

2 Good luck or bad luck? Put the words and phrases into the categories below.

good luck	bad luck
four leaf clover shooting star hear a cuckoo tiger's eye cross your fingers	walk under a ladder break a mirror black cat the number thirteen blow out all candles

Exercises

Key: 338 Key: 295

3 Superstitions/if-sentences type 1: Finish the sentences using the phrases in the box.

1. If you throw broken dishes at the houses of friends and family on New Year's Eve, they will have good luck in the New Year.
2. If you open and close scissors without cutting anything, you will have bad luck.
3. If you put your bread upside-down on the table, you will be hungry.
4. If you let your wallet or purse hit the floor, you will lose money.
5. If you eat 12 grapes one after another when the clock strikes 12 on New Year's Eve, you will have good luck for twelve months.
6. If you go to sleep with a fan* on in your room, it will kill you.
7. If bird droppings** land on you, you will be rich.

*Ventilator **Kot

you will be hungry. • it will kill you. • they will have good luck in the New Year. • you will be rich. • you will lose money. • you will have bad luck. • you will have good luck for twelve months.

Now match the superstitions with the countries where they come from. Guess! Then listen and check your answers.

France: 3 Russia: 7 Denmark: 1 South Korea: 6
Spain: 5 Egypt: 2 Brazil: 4

4 Modal verbs must/have to: Rewrite the sentence "Andrea wears something blue at her wedding." using the correct forms of must or have to.

Key: 473

Present tense	1. Ann must wear something blue at her wedding. 2. Ann has to wear something blue at her wedding.
Past tense	Ann had to wear something blue at her wedding.
Present Perfect Tense	Ann has had to wear something blue at her wedding.
Will-future	Ann will have to wear something blue at her wedding.

5 If-sentences type 1: Complete the sentences.

1. If it rains (rain) tomorrow, they will stay at home.
2. I will have good luck if I see a shooting star.
3. If people throw rice at a wedding, the couple will have (have) many children.
4. Her good luck will continue if she knocks on wood.
5. If we have time, we will go to the cinema tonight.

6 Writing: Write a text about the rules in your house. Write about

- what you have to do
- what you don't have to do
- what you mustn't do (= aren't allowed to do)

Brain teaser

Key: 707

7 Listening comprehension: Listen to Peter's story about his terrible day and tick the correct answers.

1. Peter's alarm clock didn't ring
   - [ ] last Thursday. [x] last Friday. [ ] last Tuesday.
2. When the boy prepared breakfast,
   - [ ] his mum broke a cup. [x] his mum cleaned up the mess. [ ] his mum smashed an egg.
3. Before Peter went to the bus stop, he was looking for his
   - [ ] school bag. [ ] test book. [x] lucky stone.
4. He arrived at school
   - [x] 20 minute late. [ ] 30 minutes late. [ ] 40 minutes late.
5. After school the boy had to walk home because
   - [ ] he had missed the bus. [ ] it was raining. [x] the bus had broken down.
6. He got home
   - [x] totally wet. [ ] very dirty. [ ] dry.
7. The fridge was all empty because
   - [ ] nobody had done the shopping. [x] his sister's classmates had been there. [ ] his sister had eaten up everything.

Warming up

1 Vocabulary: Think of things you dream about and write a word with each letter. Then do the same with "dilemma" but here the letters can also be in the middle of the words

D ____________ ____________D____________
R ____________ ____________I____________
E ____________ ____________L____________
A ____________ ____________E____________
M ____________ ____________M____________
S ____________ ____________M____________
Individuelle Lösung ____________A____________

Exercises

2 Past participles: Put the word halves together to find out the past participles. Then write them down.

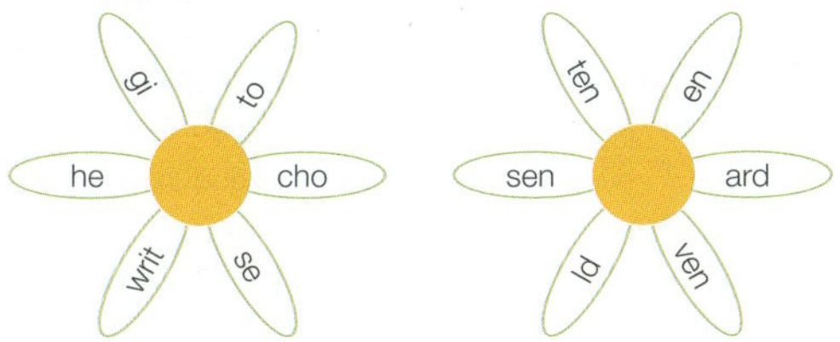

chosen
seen
written
heard
given
told

3 Past perfect tense: Fill in the past perfect forms of the verbs in brackets. Here are some sentences about dreams people had.

Key: 298

1. Kate's dream: After she had met ____________ (meet) Tom Cruise, they got married and had three children.
2. Eve's dream: She worked as a model because she had taken part ____________ (take part) in a talent show.
3. Ethan's dream: Before the police arrived, he had robbed ____________ (rob) the bank and (had) escaped ____________ (escape).
4. Luke's dream: He landed on the moon and took a walk there after he had flown ____________ (fly) into space.
5. Jenny's dream: She travelled around the world because she had won ____________ (win) the lottery.

4 If-sentences – type 2: Choose a), b) or c) to finish the sentences.

Key: 802

1.	If I	(a) remembered	b. remember	c. would remember	my dream, I would tell it to you.
2.	What	a. did	b. do	(c) would	you do if you found a bag full of money?
3.	Laura	a. were	b. was	(c) would be	very happy if Peter left his girlfriend.
4.	If they	a. would meet	(b) met	c. meet	a famous pop star, they wouldn't know what to say.

5 Past perfect tense: Matt's dream – Look at the pictures and complete the sentences with the verbs in past or past perfect tense.

Key: 507

Last night Matt had ____________ (have) an exciting dream. After he had missed ____________ (miss) the train, he followed ____________ (follow) it in a hot air balloon and flew ____________ (fly) on a snow-covered mountain. On top of the mountain Matt put ____________ (put) on his skis. After he had gone ____________ (go) downhill, he jumped ____________ (jump) on a ship. He had got off ____________ (get off) the ship, before he took ____________ (take) a motorbike. As fast as he could ____________ (can), he went ____________ (go) to the station where the train he had missed ____________ (miss) was waiting. In the morning Matt's mother woke him up ____________ (wake him up) and he felt ____________ (feel) sad because it had only been ____________ (only be) a dream.

6 Writing: Write the answer that the agony aunt* wrote to Vanessa. In your letter

- tell Vanessa what you think about her problem
- give her some advice what she should do
- tell her what she shouldn't do

Brain teaser

7 Reading comprehension: The following problem letter that Vanessa wrote to an agony aunt* is in jumbled order. Put it into the correct order, then listen and check.

Key: 694

*Kummerkastentante

6	They also make fun of my clothes and my hairstyle, but they only do it when the teacher isn't around.
9	Vanessa
4	They are always very busy and have enough problems themselves.
1	**Dear Agony aunt,**
7	The other classmates don't seem to like me either. So I never speak to anyone.
5	At my new school there are two boys who keep calling me names and the others love every time they do it.
8	I feel really depressed and I don't want to go to school anymore. What should I do? Please help me.
2	I'm a 13-year-old girl and I'm having a lot of problems at the moment. I don't know who to turn to for help.
3	Six months ago we moved to a new town and my parents started new jobs.

Dear Agony aunt,
I'm a 13-year-old girl and I'm having a lot of problems at the moment. I don't know who to turn to for help. Six months ago we moved to a new town and my parents started new jobs. They are always very busy and have enough problems themselves. At my new school there are two boys who keep calling me names and the others laugh every time they do it. They also make fun of my clothes and my hairstyle, but they only do it when the teacher isn't around. The other classmates don't seem to like me either. So I never speak to anyone. I feel really depressed and I don't want to go to school anymore. What should I do? Please help me.
Vanessa

1 Wordsearch: Find 16 words about travelling, stories, films and superstitions (four words each).

T	R	O	P	S	S	A	P	C	A	G	V	M	S	I
E	G	S	Y	M	O	P	A	F	K	N	P	I	O	C
U	S	Y	O	O	Y	M	E	L	N	I	R	R	U	A
Z	S	N	T	K	P	S	J	I	A	D	R	R	V	E
P	B	T	J	S	R	O	T	C	A	D	O	O	E	X
X	A	Z	I	V	I	M	D	E	U	E	D	R	N	V
T	E	T	R	P	V	U	I	I	R	W	A	E	I	C
P	E	S	N	O	R	K	E	L	L	I	N	G	R	F
U	U	W	R	W	T	F	R	I	S	C	O	D	S	C
S	C	R	E	A	M	C	H	I	U	Z	V	U	O	D
N	L	F	A	N	R	A	E	R	L	D	X	U	S	B
O	H	T	X	U	L	E	L	R	N	T	K	N	E	Z
J	W	S	W	I	P	Y	G	P	I	O	C	U	F	F
H	W	H	I	E	A	P	E	O	G	D	U	D	I	F
F	P	D	H	R	L	X	G	E	C	Y	L	M	Q	L

Travelling: snorkelling, campsite, passport, souvenirs

Stories: tattoo, mysterious, curly, slim

Films: director, scream, actor, DVD

Superstitions: ladder, mirror, luck, wedding

2 Word order: Put the words in the correct order.

1. cinema | is | of | who | girl | is | in | the | cousin | front | The | my | waiting
   The girl who is waiting in front of the cinema is my cousin.
2. wasn't | some | wanted | any | there | eat | cream | We | to | but | left | ice
   We wanted to eat some ice cream but there wasn't any left.
3. than | your | interesting | book | mine? | Was | more
   Was your book more interesting than mine?
4. her | play | with | had | went | to | her | After | exercises, | she | out | she | friends | finished
   After she had finished her exercises, she went out to play with her friends.

3 If sentences 1 and 2: Match the sentence halves.

1. If he loved her, he
2. If I was a teacher, I
3. If you go to England, you
4. If they took the plane, they
5. If she doesn't help her dad, he
6. If we don't hurry up, we

a. will be very angry.
b. would have to pay more.
c. will have to speak English.
d. won't be there in time.
e. would buy her a diamond ring.
f. wouldn't give any homework.

4 Mixed tenses: Fill in present simple or continuous, past simple or continuous or past perfect tense. Then listen and check.

Key: 535

Sally: Hello?
Harry: Hi, Sally, this is (be) Harry. What are you doing (you/do)?
Sally: I'm watching (I/watch) Harry Potter.
Harry: Were you not watching (you/not watch) it when I called (call) you yesterday?
Sally: Yes, that 's (be) true. I love (love) Harry Potter. I watch (watch) it every day. And what are you doing (you/do)?
Harry: Nothing. After I had phoned (phone) you yesterday, I wanted (want) to rent a Harry Potter DVD but I couldn't get (cannot get) one. Can / Could (can) I come over to your place to watch the film with you?
Sally: Sure, no problem. Bring along some crisps.

5 Modal verbs: Your English teacher is asking a lot of questions. Fill in the correct form and answer the questions so that they are true for you. Use present or past tense.

1. Can you ski? Yes, I can. / No, I can't. (can)
2. Did you have to go to bed early when you were eight years old? (must) Yes, I did. / No, I didn't.
3. Are you allowed to eat lots of sweets? (you/allowed to) Yes, I am. / No, I'm not.
4. Do you have to help your mother with the housework? (must) Yes, I do. / No, I don't.
5. Were you able to / Could you speak English when you were three years old? (can) Yes, I was. / No, I wasn't. / Yes, I could. / No, I couldn't.

6 Dilemmas and dreams: Finish the sentences to express what you would do.

Dilemmas: Examples:
If I broke my friend's favourite CD or DVD, I would buy a new one.
If my dog ate my English homework, I would be angry.
My father would be very angry if I got bad marks.

Dreams: Examples:
One of my biggest dreams would come true if I won the lottery.

If I were a millionaire, I would live in a big house.
If I met the boy / girl of my dreams, I would marry him / her.

7 If-sentences 1 and 2: Put the verbs in brackets into the correct form.

A: Joe, what would you do (do) if you were (be) rich?
B: Let me think. I would buy (buy) a Ferrari, a helicopter and a nice house.
A: And would you give (give) part of the money to your friends too if you had (have) enough of it?
B: No, I wouldn't do (not do) so even if I was (be) a millionaire.
A: If you are not nice (not be nice) to your friends, you will lose (lose) them.
B: I don't need friends who are only interested in my money.

Warming up

1 London sights: Match the pictures and the words.

Tower Bridge • London Eye • Buckingham Palace • Big Ben • Trafalgar Square • St. Paul's Cathedral

1. Trafalgar Square

2. London Eye

3. Tower Bridge

3. St. Paul's Cathedral

5. Big Ben

6. Buckingham Palace

Exercises

2 Present perfect tense domino: Write down the past participles that are hidden in the four domino snakes. The last letter of a word is also the first letter of the next one.

1. brought told drunk known
2. swam made eaten
3. woken up put thought taken
4. rung got taught thrown

3 Present perfect tense – for or since? Circle the correct word.

Key: 906

1. My uncle has lived in Oxford Street for / since twenty years.
2. I haven't spoken German for / since I arrived in London.
3. Buckingham Palace has been the official residence of Britain's monarchs for / since 1837.
4. I have queued* for / since two hours to get tickets for the London Eye.
5. Janet hasn't seen her friends from London for / since last Christmas.
6. Big Ben has been one of the world's most famous tourist attractions for / since many years.

*sich anstellen

4 Present perfect tense: Put the verbs in brackets into the present perfect tense.

1. Look! I have just bought (just/buy) tickets for Madame Tussaud's.
2. Have you ever seen (you/ever/see) a musical in London?
3. Richard hasn't visited (not/visit) the Tower of London yet.
4. Lorna and Kate have been (be) to London several times but they have never gone (never/go) to any of the street markets there.
5. Has Claire already finished (Claire/already/finish) her shopping expedition?

5 Sentence starters: Complete the text with the words from the box. Then listen and check.

Key: 488 Key: 809

then • next • last April • afterwards • on the third day • finally • first • the next day • after • so

Last April we flew to London. First we went to our hotel to check in and get rid of our luggage, then we started our visit with a sightseeing tour. After we had hopped on and off a double decker bus, we got tired and hungry. So we decided to eat fish and chips in a small restaurant where my dad spent a fortune*! Next, we visited the London Dungeon which was quite scary. The next day we went to Madame Tussaud's but we had to queue for more than an hour. Afterwards my mother and my sister wanted to go shopping in Oxford Street. We bought some souvenirs, CDs and magazines. When we finally went back to Austria on the third day, we took a ride on the London Eye. London is great!

*Vermögen

6 Writing: Write an e-mail to a friend about a trip to London. In your e-mail say

- where you went and which sights you visited
- what you liked most about London
- what you didn't like

Brain teaser

7 Present perfect or past tense? Fill in the correct form of the verbs in brackets.

Jane: How was (be) London?
Neil: Great! On our first day we went (go) to the British Museum.
Jane: How did you get (you/get) there?
Neil: We took (take) the Circle Line and changed (change) at Notting Hill Gate. We got off (get off) at Tottenham Court Road.
Jane: Did you go (You go) shopping after the museum? Some souvenirs for your family?
Neil: No, I hate shopping, especially souvenirs. My dad brought along (bring along) a T-shirt for me when he worked (work) in London two years ago but I have never worn (never/wear) it.
Jane: Have you ever been (You ever be) to the Sea Life London Aquarium?
Neil: No, I I've been (be) to London five times and I know that it opened (open) in 1997 but I haven't visited (not/visit) it yet.
Jane: You have to go there. It's amazing.

Warming up

1 Opinions: Cross out the phrases that don't express one's opinion.

If you ask me — ~~I'd like to~~ — I think — In my opinion — I believe — ~~I want~~ — ~~I can~~ — I don't think

Exercises

2 California Quiz: Tick the correct answer. Then listen and check.

Key: 282

1. What is the capital of California?
   - [ ] Los Angeles (H)
   - [ ] San Francisco (S)
   - [x] Sacramento (V)
2. What ocean borders California on the west?
   - [ ] the Atlantic Ocean (O)
   - [x] the Pacific Ocean (E)
   - [ ] the Indian Ocean (A)
3. Which sight is in San Francisco?
   - [ ] Statue of Liberty (L)
   - [x] Alcatraz (N)
   - [ ] Walk of Fame (M)
4. Which state is larger? California or Texas?
   - [x] Texas (I)
   - [ ] California (L)
5. Which bridge is not in California?
   - [x] the Brooklyn Bridge (C)
   - [ ] the Bay Bridge (S)
   - [ ] the Golden Gate Bridge (E)
6. Which state has more people? California or New York?
   - [ ] New York (W)
   - [x] California (E)
7. What's the official nickname of the state of California?
   - [ ] The Sunshine State (D).
   - [ ] the Empire State (G)
   - [x] the Golden State (B)
8. What is the hottest and driest national park called?
   - [ ] Yosemite National Park (F)
   - [x] Death Valley National Park (E)
   - [ ] Joshua Tree Park (U)
9. Where will you not meet Mickey Mouse?
   - [ ] at Disneyland (E)
   - [ ] in Anaheim (O)
   - [x] in Monterey (A)
10. Where do lots of actors, producers and film directors live?
    - [ ] in Hollywood (T)
    - [x] in Beverly Hills (C)
    - [ ] in Palm Springs (N)
11. Who was Governor of California from 2003–2011?
    - [ ] Clint Eastwood (Y)
    - [ ] Bruce Willis (D)
    - [x] Arnold Schwarzenegger (H)

Put all the letters together. Which word do you get? V E N I C E B E A C H

3 Present perfect continuous: Look at the pictures and write sentences in the present perfect continuous. Use the phrases from the box.

sleep for nearly two hours • study for their maths test since 2 p.m. • wait for 40 minutes • smoke for over twenty years • rain since Monday

1. Matthew has been waiting for 40 minutes.

2. The baby has been sleeping for nearly two hours.

3. Maria and Paul have been studying for their maths test since 2 pm.

4. In 1995 California banned smoking. In the same year Mr Smith started to smoke. So Mr Smith has been smoking for over twenty years.

5. It has been raining since Monday.

4 Your opinion: Look at exercise 3 again and give your opinion on the situations. What do you think will happen? What should the people do?

1. I think Matthew Individuell (z.B: I think Matthew should go home and tell his friend that he is angry.
2. If you ask me, the baby will wake up in a minute.
3. In my opinion Maria and Paul should stop learning and go to bed.
4. I don't think Mr Smith lives a healthy life. He should stop smoking.
5. I think the rain is good for our garden.

5 Writing: Your class is planning to go on a language trip. Some of your classmates would like to go to California, others prefer Cambridge. Write an e-mail to them in which you

- say what you like about California
- mention the disadvantages of a language trip to the USA
- express your personal opinion

Brain teaser

6 Present perfect simple or continuous? Complete Steven's e-mail from California with the correct form of the verbs.

Hi Steven,

We have been travelling (travel) around California for about two weeks now and the sun has been shining (shine) all the time. We're in Los Angeles at the moment and I can tell you I have never seen (never see) such an exciting city – Hollywood, Walk of Fame, Venice Beach, Beverly Hills, Universal Studios, Disneyland, Paul Getty Museum – it's amazing. I'm so glad Michael is here with me because we have known (know) each other for ages. He's so much fun.

I have been looking for (look for) a nice present for you but I haven't found (find) one yet. Don't worry, I'll get you something special.

I wish you were here.

CU soon,

William

Warming up

1 Wordsearch: Find 14 words that have to do with music. The first three letters are given.

K	E	Y	Q	Y	K	G	S	D	T	M	C
C	Q	E	F	T	D	O	N	N	A	H	A
O	L	K	T	M	U	O	E	O	A	T	L
N	L	C	F	N	U	M	L	R	S	Y	B
C	H	O	D	F	U	S	T	E	M	H	U
E	H	J	T	R	U	S	I	X	M	R	M
R	R	C	T	A	E	P	G	C	P	T	H
T	L	S	R	E	C	O	R	D	I	N	G
Q	N	I	C	S	T	U	D	I	O	A	U
I	G	D	N	A	B	H	C	O	Z	D	N
R	M	P	L	J	T	Z	A	V	H	Z	Q
S	C	I	R	Y	L	P	E	U	V	H	N

ALB U M
BAN D
CHA R T S
CON C E R T
DIS C J O C K E Y
INS T R U M E N T
LYR I C S
MEL O D Y
MUS I C I A N
REC O R D I N G
RHY T H M

SOU N D
SON G
STU D I O

Exercises

2 Passive: Are the sentences active or passive? Tick the right box.

Key: 137

	A	P
1. The concert was cancelled because of rain.		x
2. I was listening to pop music on my iPod.	x	
3. Are CDs made from plastic?		x
4. Britney Spears was born in 1981.		x
5. They are the best singers I know.	x	
6. A song isn't easily produced.		x

3 Passive: How your music career starts. Put the sentences into the present simple passive.

1. You form a band — A band is formed.
2. You write the lyrics. — The lyrics are written.
3. You rehearse* all the songs. — All the songs are rehearsed.
4. You invite your friends to a concert. — Your friends are invited to a concert.
5. You record a CD. — A CD is recorded.
6. You release it. — It is released.
7. Thousands of people buy it. — It is bought by thousands of people.

*proben

4 Links: Match the sentence halves.

Key: 591

1. Do you like techno	a. and so he really got better soon.
2. I started to learn how to play the violin when I was eight	b. but I gave up at eleven.
3. I stopped playing the violin	c. or do you prefer hip hop?
4. First the melody must be found	d. because she has got a brilliant voice.
5. Michael took piano lessons,	e. and then the lyrics are written.
6. Sharon won the talent show	f. or is he a singer?
7. I really love heavy metal	g. but I hate jazz.
8. Does Daniel work as a disc jockey	h. because it was so difficult.

5 Vocabulary: Put the words from the box into the right category.

techno • disc jockey • sound engineer • flute • reggae • classical music • piano • music shop assistant • guitar • dancer • heavy metal • keyboard • songwriter • pop • drums • producer • hip hop • trumpet • jazz • violin • singer

Musical instruments	Types of music	Music industry jobs
flute, piano, guitar, keyboard	techno, reggae, classical	disc jockey, sound engineer
drums, trumpet, violin	heavy metal, pop, hip hop	music shop assistant, dancer
	jazz	songwriter, producer, singer

6 Passive: Complete the interview with the correct form of the verbs in the passive. Then listen and check.

Key: 404

Andrea: Peter, what's your favourite band?
Peter: The Thunderbirds.
Andrea: I've never heard of them. Who are they?
Peter: They are four boys from Linz and their band was formed (form) in 2007. Their first concert was played (play) in a small pub in Linz in the same year.
Andrea: Do they sing in German or English?
Peter: At the beginning their lyrics were written (write) in German and their first album was released (release) in German too. But now all their songs are sung (sing) in English so that they are understood (understand) worldwide.
Andrea: How many albums have been released so far?
Peter: Three. They can only be bought (buy) directly from them.

7 Writing: Write a blog about

- your favourite band
- the songs you like
- your favourite types of music

Brain teaser

8 Jumbled interview: Unscramble the words. Then put the interview in order. Listen to check your answers.

Key: 168

[3] Interviewer: I see. When did you release your debut album (luabm)?
[7] Interviewer: What about your private lives? Your fans (nasf) would like to be informed about your partners, your stories …
[5] Interviewer: How many albums have you released so far?
[1] Interviewer: Welcome Niall, Zayn, Liam, Harry and Louis! Tell me, how were you discovered (vosedicrde)?
[8] One Direction: We'd like to keep that to ourselves. Bye!
[4] One Direction: Our first album was released (aeredsle) in 2011.
[2] One Direction: We took part in the TV talent show (stnolweath) The X Factor. That was in 2010.
[6] One Direction: Four (rouf), but we're already working on our fifth album.

Fun pages 2

1 Riddles: Find the answers.

1. What month do soldiers hate?
   M a r c h
2. What stays hot even if put in a refrigerator?
   (It's not salt.) p e p p e r
3. Why should we never ask balloons for advice?
   Because they are full of h o t a i r.
4. What will make more noise in your house than a dog?
   t w o d o g s

5. What weather do mice and rats fear?
   When it is raining c a t s and d o g s
6. What can't be used unless broken?
   (You can eat them.) e g g s

2 Read the stories and try to answer the questions.

1 A murderer is sentenced to death*. He has to choose between three rooms. The first is full of fires, the second is full of gangsters with loaded guns, and the third is full of lions that haven't eaten anything for 3 years. Which room is safest for him?

2 A woman was driving a black car. The lights of the car were off. The moon wasn't shining. A black cat was in the middle of the road. How did the woman know to stop in front of the cat?

3 Two girls ate dinner together. They both ordered ice tea. One girl drank them very fast and drank three of them in the time it took the other girl to drink one. The girl who drank one died while the other survived. All of the drinks were poisoned. Why did the girl that drank more ice tea survive?

4 A man and his son are in a terrible accident and are rushed to the hospital in intensive care. The doctor looks at the boy and exclaims "I can't operate on this boy, he's my son!" How could this be?

*zum Tode verurteilt

1 The third room. Lions that haven't eaten in three years are dead.

2 It was a very bright and sunny day.

3 *The poison was in the middle of the ice.*

4 *The doctor is the boy's mother.*

3 Do the logical puzzle.

It's party time!
At Peter's birthday party his friends each gave him a different present and then they were given a glass of a different colour. Also they were each given a different bar of chocolate. Find out who had what.

Name: Andy, Daniel, William, Tom
Present: box of Lego, book, sweets, toy car
Glass: blue, green, red, yellow
Chocolate: Bounty, Mars, Snickers, Twix

Name	Present	Glass	Chocolate bar
Andy	book	red	Mars
Daniel	box of Lego	yellow	Twix
William	sweets	green	Bounty
Tom	toy car	blue	Snickers

1. Tom was not given a Twix or a red glass.
2. The Snickers was given to the boy that gave the toy car to Peter.
3. Andy gave Peter the book.
4. William was given a Bounty, but he did not give the Lego to Peter.
5. The Mars was given to the boy that also received the red glass.
6. The sweets were given by the boy who got a green glass.
7. Daniel loved the yellow glass he was given.

4 Odd one out: Cross out the wrong word.

1. ~~bus station~~ underground train taxi
2. Tower of London ~~Statue of Liberty~~ St. Paul's Cathedral Westminster Abbey
3. rain fog sunshine ~~warm~~
4. turn left go straight ahead ~~you're right~~ take the 2nd right
5. visit ~~ticket~~ buy eat

Warming up

1 Vocabulary: Are these things good or bad for the environment? Write them in the correct column.

traffic • rainforest • pollution • recycling • pesticides • waste • organic food • global warming • cycle paths • electric cars

+	–
rainforest	traffic
recycling	pollution
organic food	pesticides
cycle paths	waste
electric cars	global warming

Now add more words to the list. Individuelle Lösung

Exercises

2 Passive: Complete the leaflet about the environment with the correct passive forms.

Caring for our environment

- Tons of plastic are thrown away (throw away) every year.
- In the last few decades greenhouse gases have grown (grow) rapidly. These gases heat up the earth's surface and this results in global warming.
- One third of humans doesn't have access to clean, fresh water. In a few years time, wars will be fought (fight) for water.
- Since 1990 half of the world's rain forests have been destroyed (destroy).

What should be done (should do)?

- Say no to plastic bags in supermarkets. Cloth bags* can be used (can use) instead.
- Drive an electric car. Do you know that the first electric car was built (build) in 1834?
- A lot of water can be saved (can save) in the household. Take a shower instead of a bath, turn the tap** off while brushing your teeth and don't wash your clothes or dishes when the machines are half-empty.
- Solar and wind energy should be used (should use) much more.
- Glass, metal and paper are recycled (recycle) easily. There are recycling bins everywhere.
- Locally produced food should be bought. (should buy).

Act now!

*Stofftaschen **Wasserhahn

Key: 178

3 Pronouns: Complete the dialogue with the correct personal (I, you, he ...), possessive (my, your, his ...) or reflexive (myself, yourself, himself) pronouns.

A: John, who does the shopping in your house?
B: I usually do it myself. When I'm busy, my wife does it. My / Our son sometimes helps me / us.
A: Do you take plastic bags at the supermarkets?
B: No, I have a big box in my car and my wife always uses her own basket.
A: What else do you do to protect our environment?
B: We always switch off the lights when we leave a room. Our kids ride their bikes to school and we also recycle glass bottles, metal and paper. In addition, we drive an electric car. We all love it.

4 Word formation

a. Find the missing nouns or verbs.

Nouns	Verbs
reduction	reduce
pollution	pollute
protection	protect
destruction	destroy
recycling	recycle

b. Now find the missing nouns or adjectives.

Nouns	Adjectives
electricity	electric, electrical
globalisation	global
environment	environmental
help	helpful
health	healthy

5 Writing: What can/should be done to protect our environment? Write an article for the school magazine. In your article write about

- what people mustn't do in order to protect our environment
- what every single person can/should do
- what the state should do

Brain teaser

6 Reading: Read the text and tick the correct answers.

At least nine people were killed after a series of tornadoes slammed through the Oklahoma City area Thursday, with at least 100 people injured. The heavy storm hit during the evening rush hour, caused chaos on Interstate 30, a major road connecting the east and the west of the city, and dropped so much rain on the area that streets were flooded to a depth of 4 feet.
Power utilities* Oklahoma Gas and Electric said that 200,000 customers were without power in Oklahoma, Missouri and Illinois. Meanwhile, according to the National Weather Service, about 30 people were rescued from areas cut off by rising water. The region was lucky because the storm touched down mostly in rural areas and missed central Oklahoma City. On average, there are more than 1,200 tornadoes in the U.S. every year and most are relatively small. Of the 60 worst tornadoes to hit since 1950, Oklahoma and Alabama have been hit the most – seven times each.

*Energieversorgungsunternehmen

1. Where would you find such a text?
   - ☐ in a geography school textbook
   - ☐ in a guidebook about Oklahoma
   - ☒ in a newspaper

2. What is the best headline for this text?
   - ☐ Interstate 30 is an important road
   - ☒ At least nine dead after tornadoes hit Oklahoma City
   - ☐ 30 people rescued

Warming up

1 Vocabulary: Put the following words into alphabetical order.

love • respect • fun • laugh • fair • secret • lie • help • close • understanding • busy • ignore • hurt • honest • important • date • favourite • listen • happy • reliable • true

busy, close, date, fair, favourite, fun, happy, help, honest, hurt, ignore, important, laugh, lie, listen, love, reliable, respect, secret, true, understanding

Exercises

Key: 670

2 Prepositions: Match the sentences to the pictures. Then complete the sentences below.

A

B

C

D

1. A: Emily's birthday is on Thursday, but her party is on Saturday. Do you know when it starts? B
   B: I think at 5 pm. Is Michael going to the party?
   A: I'm afraid he's not invited.
2. This is Barbara's boyfriend over there in front of the flower shop. He is tall and dark-haired and he is standing between two blond boys. Can you see him? D
3. Laura and Caroline are talking behind Patrick's back. That's really unfair. We should inform him about his "friends". C
4. Joe normally gets up at six o'clock. He goes to school by bus although* his best friend always goes by bike. A

*obwohl

3 Vocabulary: Take the words from exercise 1 and put them into the correct category. Some words can be written in two categories.

Nouns	date	favourite	fun	help	laugh
	lie	love	respect	secret	understanding
Verbs	close	date	help	hurt	ignore
	laugh	lie	listen	love	respect
Adjectives	busy	close	fair	favourite	happy
	honest	important	reliable	secret	true

4 Tenses: Write five sentences that are true for you. Use words from at least two categories for each sentence. Mind the tenses!

I / My best friend / All my friends / My parents / You — never / sometimes / always — lie / keep a secret / help / be honest with / phone — for … / since … / last year / next week

individuell (e.g. My best friend has never lied to me.)

5 Tenses: Fill in the correct form of the verbs.

I haven't seen (not see) George for three weeks. Last night he called (call) me while I was having (have) a bath. Next Saturday we are going (go) to the cinema together. I am (be) so happy!
My brother Tim, however, is trying (try) hard to find a girlfriend at the moment. He has been looking (look) for a nice girl since October but he hasn't found (not find) one yet.

6 Writing: Write a text about your best friend.

- Describe what is he or she is like.
- Say what you like doing together.
- Explain why he or she is your best friend.

Brain teaser

Key: 528

7 Listening: Listen to the quotes and proverbs about friendship and fill in the missing words.

1. Many people will walk in and out of your life, but only true friends will leave footprints in your hearts.
2. Make new friends but keep the old. One is silver and the other is gold.
3. Some friends come into your life for a reason others come in for a season.
4. Fake friends are like shadows. They follow you in the sun, but leave you in the dark.
5. Making a million friends is not a miracle. The miracle is to make a friend who will stand up for you when millions are against you.
6. Good friends are like stars. You don't always see them, but you know they are always there.

1 Vocabulary: Unscramble the words and write them down.

1. one of the sights in London — onLnod yEe — London Eye
2. musical instrument — eluft — flute
3. bicycle lane — ceylc taph — cycle path
4. a friend always keeps it — creste — secret
5. type of music — ihp poh — hip hop
6. we must protect it — vinnnereomt — environment

2 London Quiz: Write down the questions or answers about the capital of England.

QUESTIONS	ANSWERS
Which river runs through London?	The Thames.
Where does the Queen live?	In Buckingham Palace.
What's the name of the world's largest moving wheel?	London Eye.
What's the name of the underground?	The tube.
What is the world's most famous bell called?	Big Ben.
How many people live in London?	More than seven million people.

3 Vocabulary: Find the opposites.

1. sunshine — rain
2. to tell the truth — to lie
3. reality — dream
4. to destroy — to protect
5. healthy — unhealthy
6. punctual — late
7. to waste — to save
8. straight hair — curly hair

4 Tick the correct box.

The proverb* *A friend in need is a friend indeed* means

a. A real friend needs you and you need him/her.
(b.) A real friend helps you when you have a problem.
c. A real friend is not easy to find.

*Sprichwort

5 Passive: Now you are the teacher. Correct the sentences.

1. A large part of the tropical rainforests destroys each year.
   A large part of the tropical rainforests is destroyed each year.
2. If greenhouse gases don't reduce, the global temperature will rise.
   If greenhouse gases aren't reduced, the global temperature will rise.
3. Some new cycle paths built in our town last year.
   Some new cycle paths were built in our town last year.
4. Mountains of rubbish are dropping in the streets.
   Mountains of rubbish are dropped in the streets.
5. Pollution must stopped!
   Pollution must be stopped!

6 Do the crossword puzzle.

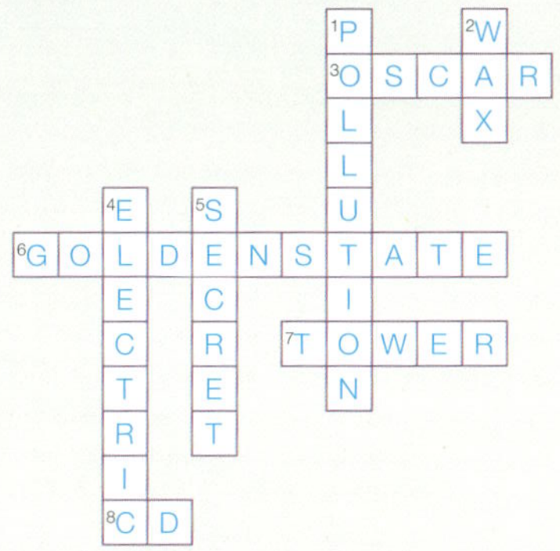

Across

3. It can be won by excellent actors and actresses.
6. It is the nickname of California.
7. The Crown Jewels are kept there.
8. It is released when all the songs are recorded.

Down

1. It must be stopped to save our planet.
2. Madame Tussauds figures are made of it.
4. Petrol is not needed for electric cars.
5. A good friend always keeps it.

Now take the following letters of the words you filled in to find out what the author of this book wants to tell you at the end of Ferienheft 3: from 2 the 1st letter, from 5 the 2nd letter, from 1 the 3rd letter, from 4 the 2nd letter, from 8 the 2nd letter, from 3 the 1st letter, from 6 the 6th letter and from 7 the 4th letter.

W E L L D O N E !!

4 Present perfect tense: Put the verbs in brackets into the present perfect tense.

1. Look! I ____________________ (just/buy) tickets for Madame Tussaud's.
2. ____________________ (you/ever/see) a musical in London?
3. Richard ____________________ (not/visit) the Tower of London yet.
4. Lorna and Kate ____________________ (be) to London several times but they ____________________ (never/go) to any of the street markets there.
5. ____________________ (Claire/already/finish) her shopping expedition?

5 Sentence starters: Complete the text with the words from the box. Then listen and check.

Key: 488 Key: 809

then • next • last April • afterwards • on the third day • finally • first • the next day • after • so

____________________ we flew to London. ____________ we went to our hotel to check in and get rid of our luggage, ____________ we started our visit with a sightseeing tour. ____________ we had hopped on and off a double decker bus, we got tired and hungry. ________ we decided to eat fish and chips in a small restaurant where my dad spent a fortune*! ____________, we visited the London Dungeon which was quite scary. ____________ we went to Madame Tussaud's but we had to queue for more than an hour. ______________ my mother and my sister wanted to go shopping in Oxford Street. We bought some souvenirs, CDs and magazines. When we ____________ went back to Austria ____________________, we took a ride on the London Eye. London is great!

*Vermögen

6 Writing: Write an e-mail to a friend about a trip to London. In your e-mail say

- where you went and which sights you visited
- what you liked most about London
- what you didn't like

Brain teaser

7 Present perfect or past tense? Fill in the correct form of the verbs in brackets.

Jane: How ________ (be) London?
Neil: Great! On our first day we __________ (go) to the British Museum.
Jane: How ________________ (you/get) there?
Neil: We __________ (take) the Circle Line and ____________ (change) at Notting Hill Gate. We ____________ (get off) at Tottenham Court Road.
Jane: ________________ (You go) shopping after the museum? Some souvenirs for your family?
Neil: No, I hate shopping, especially souvenirs. My dad ________________ (bring along) a T-shirt for me when he ____________ (work) in London two years ago but I ________________ (never/wear) it.
Jane: ____________________ (You ever be) to the Sea Life London Aquarium?
Neil: No, I ____________ (be) to London five times and I know that it ____________ (open) in 1997 but I ________________ (not/visit) it yet.
Jane: You have to go there. It's amazing.

Warming up

1 Opinions: Cross out the phrases that don't express one's opinion.

If you ask me — I'd like to — I think — In my opinion — I believe — I want — I can — I don't think

Exercises

2 California Quiz: Tick the correct answer. Then listen and check.

Key: 282

1. What is the capital of California?
   ☐ Los Angeles (H) ☐ San Francisco (S) ☐ Sacramento (V)
2. What ocean borders California on the west?
   ☐ the Atlantic Ocean (O) ☐ the Pacific Ocean (E) ☐ the Indian Ocean (A)
3. Which sight is in San Francisco?
   ☐ Statue of Liberty (L) ☐ Alcatraz (N) ☐ Walk of Fame (M)
4. Which state is larger? California or Texas?
   ☐ Texas (I) ☐ California (L)
5. Which bridge is not in California?
   ☐ the Brooklyn Bridge (C) ☐ the Bay Bridge (S) ☐ the Golden Gate Bridge (E)
6. Which state has more people? California or New York?
   ☐ New York (W) ☐ California (E)
7. What's the official nickname of the state of California?
   ☐ The Sunshine State (D). ☐ the Empire State (G) ☐ the Golden State (B)
8. What is the hottest and driest national park called?
   ☐ Yosemite National Park (F) ☐ Death Valley National Park (E) ☐ Joshua Tree Park (U)
9. Where will you not meet Mickey Mouse?
   ☐ at Disneyland (E) ☐ in Anaheim (O) ☐ in Monterey (A)
10. Where do lots of actors, producers and film directors live?
   ☐ in Hollywood (T) ☐ in Beverly Hills (C) ☐ in Palm Springs (N)
11. Who was Governor of California from 2003–2011?
   ☐ Clint Eastwood (Y) ☐ Bruce Willis (D) ☐ Arnold Schwarzenegger (H)

Put all the letters together. Which word do you get? _ _ _ _ _ _ _ _ _ _ _

3 Present perfect continuous: Look at the pictures and write sentences in the present perfect continuous. Use the phrases from the box.

sleep for nearly two hours • study for their maths test since 2 p.m. • wait for 40 minutes • smoke for over twenty years • rain since Monday

1. Matthew ______________________________

____

2. The baby ______________________________

____

3. Maria and Paul ______________________________

____

4. In 1995 California banned smoking. In the same year Mr Smith started to smoke. So ______________________________

5. It ______________________________

____

4 Your opinion: Look at exercise 3 again and give your opinion on the situations. What do you think will happen? What should the people do?

1. I think Matthew ______________________________
2. If you ask me, ______________________________
3. ______________________________
4. ______________________________
5. ______________________________

5 Writing: Your class is planning to go on a language trip. Some of your classmates would like to go to California, others prefer Cambridge. Write an e-mail to them in which you

- say what you like about California
- mention the disadvantages of a language trip to the USA
- express your personal opinion

Brain teaser

6 Present perfect simple or continuous? Complete Steven's e-mail from California with the correct form of the verbs.

Hi Steven,

We ______________________ (travel) around California for about two weeks now and the sun ______________________ (shine) all the time. We're in Los Angeles at the moment and I can tell you I ______________________ (never see) such an exciting city – Hollywood, Walk of Fame, Venice Beach, Beverly Hills, Universal Studios, Disneyland, Paul Getty Museum – it's amazing. I'm so glad Michael is here with me because we ______________________ (know) each other for ages. He's so much fun.

I ______________________ (look for) a nice present for you but I ______________________ (find) one yet. Don't worry, I'll get you something special.

I wish you were here.

CU soon,

William

Warming up

1 Wordsearch: Find 14 words that have to do with music. The first three letters are given.

K	E	Y	Q	Y	K	G	S	D	T	M	C
C	Q	E	F	T	D	O	N	N	A	H	A
O	L	K	T	M	U	O	E	O	A	T	L
N	L	C	F	N	U	M	L	R	S	Y	B
C	H	O	D	F	U	S	T	E	M	H	U
E	H	J	T	R	U	S	I	X	M	R	M
R	R	C	T	A	E	P	G	C	P	T	H
T	L	S	R	E	C	O	R	D	I	N	G
Q	N	I	C	S	T	U	D	I	O	A	U
I	G	D	N	A	B	H	C	O	Z	D	N
R	M	P	L	J	T	Z	A	V	H	Z	Q
S	C	I	R	Y	L	P	E	U	V	H	N

ALB _ _
BAN _
CHA _ _ _
CON _ _ _ _
DIS _ _ _ _ _ _ _ _
INS _ _ _ _ _ _ _
LYR _ _ _
MEL _ _ _
MUS _ _ _ _ _
REC _ _ _ _ _ _
RHY _ _ _
SOU _ _
SON _
STU _ _ _

Exercises

Key: 137

2 Passive: Are the sentences active or passive? Tick the right box.

	A	P
1. The concert was cancelled because of rain.		
2. I was listening to pop music on my iPod.		
3. Are CDs made from plastic?		

	A	P
4. Britney Spears was born in 1981.		
5. They are the best singers I know.		
6. A song isn't easily produced.		

3 Passive: How your music career starts. Put the sentences into the present simple passive.

1. You form a band — *A band is formed.*
2. You write the lyrics. ______
3. You rehearse* all the songs. ______
4. You invite your friends to a concert. ______
5. You record a CD. ______
6. You release it. ______
7. Thousands of people buy it. ______

*proben

4 Links: Match the sentence halves.

Key: 591

1. Do you like techno
2. I started to learn how to play the violin when I was eight
3. I stopped playing the violin
4. First the melody must be found
5. Michael took piano lessons,
6. Sharon won the talent show
7. I really love heavy metal
8. Does Daniel work as a disc jockey

a. and so he really got better soon.
b. but I gave up at eleven.
c. or do you prefer hip hop?
d. because she has got a brilliant voice.
e. and then the lyrics are written.
f. or is he a singer?
g. but I hate jazz.
h. because it was so difficult.

5 Vocabulary: Put the words from the box into the right category.

techno • disc jockey • sound engineer • flute • reggae • classical music • piano • music shop assistant • guitar • dancer • heavy metal • keyboard • songwriter • pop • drums • producer • hip hop • trumpet • jazz • violin • singer

Musical instruments	Types of music	Music industry jobs

6 Passive: Complete the interview with the correct form of the verbs in the passive. Then listen and check.

Key: 404

Andrea: Peter, what's your favourite band?
Peter: The Thunderbirds.
Andrea: I've never heard of them. Who are they?
Peter: They are four boys from Linz and their band ____________ (form) in 2007. Their first concert ____________ (play) in a small pub in Linz in the same year.
Andrea: Do they sing in German or English?
Peter: At the beginning their lyrics ____________ (write) in German and their first album ____________ (release) in German too. But now all their songs ____________ (sing) in English so that they ____________ (understand) worldwide.
Andrea: How many albums have been released so far?
Peter: Three. They can only ____________ (buy) directly from them.

7 Writing: Write a blog about

- your favourite band
- the songs you like
- your favourite types of music

Brain teaser

8 Jumbled interview: Unscramble the words. Then put the interview in order. Listen to check your answers.

Key: 168

☐ Interviewer: I see. When did you release your debut ____________ (luabm)?
☐ Interviewer: What about your private lives? Your ____________ (nasf) would like to be informed about your partners, your stories …
☐ Interviewer: How many albums have you released so far?
☐ Interviewer: Welcome Niall, Zayn, Liam, Harry and Louis! Tell me, how were you ____________ (vosedicrde)?
☐ One Direction: We'd like to keep that to ourselves. Bye!
☐ One Direction: Our first album was ____________ (aeredsle) in 2011.
☐ One Direction: We took part in the TV ____________ ____________ (stnolweath) The X Factor. That was in 2010.
☐ One Direction: ____________ (rouf), but we're already working on our fifth album.

Fun pages 2

1 Riddles: Find the answers.

1. What month do soldiers hate?
   M _ _ _ _
2. What stays hot even if put in a refrigerator?
   (It's not salt.) _ _ _ _ _ _ _
3. Why should we never ask balloons for advice?
   Because they are full of h _ _ a _ _.
4. What will make more noise in your house than a dog?
   t _ _ d _ _ _
5. What weather do mice and rats fear?
   When it is raining _ _ _ _ and _ _ _ _ _

6. What can't be used unless broken?
   (You can eat them.) e _ _ _

2 Read the stories and try to answer the questions.

1 A murderer is sentenced to death*. He has to choose between three rooms. The first is full of fires, the second is full of gangsters with loaded guns, and the third is full of lions that haven't eaten anything for 3 years. Which room is safest for him?

2 A woman was driving a black car. The lights of the car were off. The moon wasn't shining. A black cat was in the middle of the road. How did the woman know to stop in front of the cat?

3 Two girls ate dinner together. They both ordered ice tea. One girl drank them very fast and drank three of them in the time it took the other girl to drink one. The girl who drank one died while the other survived. All of the drinks were poisoned. Why did the girl that drank more ice tea survive?

4 A man and his son are in a terrible accident and are rushed to the hospital in intensive care. The doctor looks at the boy and exclaims "I can't operate on this boy, he's my son!" How could this be?

*zum Tode verurteilt

The third room. Lions that haven't eaten in three years are dead.

It was a very bright and sunny day.

The poison was in the middle of the ice.

The doctor is the boy's mother.

3 Do the logical puzzle.

It's party time!

At Peter's birthday party his friends each gave him a different present and then they were given a glass of a different colour. Also they were each given a different bar of chocolate. Find out who had what.

Name: Andy, Daniel, William, Tom
Present: box of Lego, book, sweets, toy car
Glass: blue, green, red, yellow
Chocolate: Bounty, Mars, Snickers, Twix

Name	Present	Glass	Chocolate bar

1. Tom was not given a Twix or a red glass.
2. The Snickers was given to the boy that gave the toy car to Peter.
3. Andy gave Peter the book.
4. William was given a Bounty, but he did not give the Lego to Peter.
5. The Mars was given to the boy that also received the red glass.
6. The sweets were given by the boy who got a green glass.
7. Daniel loved the yellow glass he was given.

4 Odd one out: Cross out the wrong word.

1. bus station underground train taxi
2. Tower of London Statue of Liberty St. Paul's Cathedral Westminster Abbey
3. rain fog sunshine warm
4. turn left go straight ahead you're right take the 2nd right
5. visit ticket buy eat

Warming up

1 Vocabulary: Are these things good or bad for the environment? Write them in the correct column.

traffic • rainforest • pollution • recycling • pesticides • waste • organic food • global warming • cycle paths • electric cars

+	−
rainforest	traffic
recycling	pollution
organic food	pesticides
cycle paths	waste
electric cars.	global warming

Now add more words to the list.

Exercises

2 Passive: Complete the leaflet about the environment with the correct passive forms.

Caring for our environment

- Tons of plastic are thrown (throw away) every year.
- In the last few decades greenhouse gases have grown (grow) rapidly. These gases heat up the earth's surface and this results in global warming.
- One third of humans doesn't have access to clean, fresh water. In a few years time, wars are fought (fight) for water.
- Since 1990 half of the world's rain forests is destroyed (destroy).

What should we do (should do)?

- Say no to plastic bags in supermarkets. Cloth bags* can be used (can use) instead.
- Drive an electric car. Do you know that the first electric car was built (build) in 1834?
- A lot of water could be saved (can save) in the household. Take a shower instead of a bath, turn the tap** off while brushing your teeth and don't wash your clothes or dishes when the machines are half-empty.
- Solar and wind energy should be used (should use) much more.
- Glass, metal and paper should be recycled (recycle) easily. There are recycling bins everywhere.
- Locally produced food should be bought (should buy).

Act now!

* Stofftaschen ** Wasserhahn

3 Pronouns: Complete the dialogue with the correct personal (I, you, he ...), possessive (my, your, his ...) or reflexive (myself, yourself, himself) pronouns.

Key: 178

A: John, who does the shopping in ______________ house?

B: I usually do it ______________ . When I'm busy, _________ wife does it. ______________ son sometimes helps ______________.

A: Do you take plastic bags at the supermarkets?

B: No, I have a big box in my car and ____________ wife always uses ____________ own basket.

A: What else do you do to protect ____________ environment?

B: We always switch off the lights when we leave a room. ____________ kids ride ____________ bikes to school and ____________ also recycle glass bottles, metal and paper. In addition, we drive an electric car. We all love ____________.

4 Word formation

a. Find the missing nouns or verbs.

Nouns	Verbs
reduction	
	pollute
	protect
destruction	
	recycle

b. Now find the missing nouns or adjectives.

Nouns	Adjectives
electricity	
globalisation	
	environmental
	helpful
health	

5 Writing: What can/should be done to protect our environment? Write an article for the school magazine. In your article write about

- what people mustn't do in order to protect our environment
- what every single person can/should do
- what the state should do

Brain teaser

6 Reading: Read the text and tick the correct answers.

At least nine people were killed after a series of tornadoes slammed through the Oklahoma City area Thursday, with at least 100 people injured. The heavy storm hit during the evening rush hour, caused chaos on Interstate 30, a major road connecting the east and the west of the city, and dropped so much rain on the area that streets were flooded to a depth of 4 feet.
Power utilities* Oklahoma Gas and Electric said that 200,000 customers were without power in Oklahoma, Missouri and Illinois. Meanwhile, according to the National Weather Service, about 30 people were rescued from areas cut off by rising water. The region was lucky because the storm touched down mostly in rural areas and missed central Oklahoma City. On average, there are more than 1,200 tornadoes in the U.S. every year and most are relatively small. Of the 60 worst tornadoes to hit since 1950, Oklahoma and Alabama have been hit the most – seven times each.

*Energieversorgungsunternehmen

1. Where would you find such a text?
   - ☐ in a geography school textbook
   - ☐ in a guidebook about Oklahoma
   - ☐ in a newspaper

2. What is the best headline for this text?
   - ☐ Interstate 30 is an important road
   - ☐ At least nine dead after tornadoes hit Oklahoma City
   - ☐ 30 people rescued

Warming up

1 Vocabulary: Put the following words into alphabetical order.

love • respect • fun • laugh • fair • secret • lie • help • close • understanding • busy • ignore • hurt • honest • important • date • favourite • listen • happy • reliable • true

____

____

Exercises

Key: 670

2 Prepositions: Match the sentences to the pictures. Then complete the sentences below.

A

B

C

D

1. A: Emily's ____________ is ______ Thursday, but her party is ______ Saturday.
   Do you know when it starts?
   B: I think ______ 5 pm. Is Michael going ______ the party?
   A: I'm afraid he's not invited.
2. This is Barbara's boyfriend over there ________ the flower shop. He is tall and dark-haired and he is standing ________ two blond boys. Can you see him?
3. Laura and Caroline are talking ________ Patrick's back. That's really unfair. We should inform him ________ his "friends".

4 Joe normally gets ______ ______ six o'clock. He goes ______ school ______ bus although* his best friend always goes ______ ________.

*obwohl

3 Vocabulary: Take the words from exercise 1 and put them into the correct category. Some words can be written in two categories.

Nouns					
Verbs					
Adjectives					

4 Tenses: Write five sentences that are true for you. Use words from at least two categories for each sentence. Mind the tenses!

I My best friend All my friends My parents You	never sometimes always	lie keep a secret help be honest with phone	for … since … last year next week

____

____

____

____

____

5 Tenses: Fill in the correct form of the verbs.

I ______ (not see) George for three weeks. Last night he ______(call) me while I ______ (have) a bath. Next Saturday we ______ (go) to the cinema together. I ______ (be) so happy!
My brother Tim, however, ______ (try) hard to find a girlfriend at the moment. He ______(look) for a nice girl since October but he ______ (not find) one yet.

6 Writing: Write a text about your best friend.

- Describe what is he or she is like.
- Say what you like doing together.
- Explain why he or she is your best friend.

Brain teaser

7 Listening: Listen to the quotes and proverbs about friendship and fill in the missing words.

Key: 528

1. Many people will walk in and out of your ______, but only true friends will leave ______ in your hearts.
2. Make new friends but keep the old. One is ______ and the other is ______.
3. Some friends come into your life for a ______ others come in for a ______.
4. Fake friends are like ______. They follow you in the ______, but leave you in the ______.
5. Making a million friends is not a ______. The ______ is to make a friend who will ______ when millions are against you.
6. Good friends are like ______. You don't always see them, but you ______ they are always there.

Revision 2

1 Vocabulary: Unscramble the words and write them down.

1.	one of the sights in London	onLnod yEe	______
2.	musical instrument	eluft	______
3.	bicycle lane	ceylc taph	______
4.	a friend always keeps it	creste	______
5.	type of music	ihp poh	______
6.	we must protect it	vinnnereomt	______

2 London Quiz: Write down the questions or answers about the capital of England.

QUESTIONS	ANSWERS
	The Thames.
Where does the Queen live?	
What's the name of the world's largest moving wheel?	
	The tube.
What is the world's most famous bell called?	
	More than seven million people.

3 Vocabulary: Find the opposites.

1. sunshine ______
2. to tell the truth ______
3. reality ______
4. to destroy ______
5. healthy ______
6. punctual ______
7. to waste ______
8. straight hair ______

4 Tick the correct box.

The proverb* *A friend in need is a friend indeed* means

a. A real friend needs you and you need him/her.
b. A real friend helps you when you have a problem.
c. A real friend is not easy to find.

*Sprichwort

5 Passive: Now you are the teacher. Correct the sentences.

1. A large part of the tropical rainforests destroys each year.

____

2. If greenhouse gases don't reduce, the global temperature will rise.

____

3. Some new cycle paths built in our town last year.

____

4. Mountains of rubbish are dropping in the streets.

____

5. Pollution must stopped!

____

6 Do the crossword puzzle.

Across

3. It can be won by excellent actors and actresses.
6. It is the nickname of California.
7. The Crown Jewels are kept there.
8. It is released when all the songs are recorded.

Down

1. It must be stopped to save our planet.
2. Madame Tussauds figures are made of it.
4. Petrol is not needed for ______________ cars.
5. A good friend always keeps it.

Now take the following letters of the words you filled in to find out what the author of this book wants to tell you at the end of Ferienheft 3: from 2 the 1st letter, from 5 the 2nd letter, from 1 the 3rd letter, from 4 the 2nd letter, from 8 the 2nd letter, from 3 the 1st letter, from 6 the 6th letter and from 7 the 4th letter.

_ _ _ _   _ _ _ _ !!

Tapescripts

Day 1

Exercise 3

Interviewer: Why do you like travelling?
Samantha: It is always exciting and a lot of fun. You see different places and you meet different people.
Interviewer: Where do you usually travel?
Samantha: We often go to Italy or Croatia in the summer. Or we visit a European city like Paris, Rome or London.
Interviewer: Did you take a city break last year?
Samantha: No, last year we didn't. We flew to Australia in July.That was great!
Interviewer: Wow! How long did you stay there?
Samantha: For a month. We spent one week in Sydney and one in Melbourne. Then we took the bus to Central Australia to see Ayers Rock. And after that we went snorkelling at the Great Barrier Reef. It was fantastic!
Interviewer: That sounds great.

Exercise 4

This is what you need if you want to go camping: a tent, a table, some chairs, something to eat and drink and some games for the children.
There are also rules campers have to keep in mind: don't take any jewellery or anything expensive with you. Don't go anywhere isolated, stay at campsites. Never keep any food inside your tent because it might attract animals. Take some friends with you if you like but don't ask anybody you don't really get on well with. Observe quiet hours and speed limits at the campsite. Don't give anybody any reason to be angry with you.

Day 2

Exercise 2

When I saw Kevin last week, I couldn't believe my eyes. He was sitting in a bar with two young men. They were drinking whisky and smoking cigars. Kevin was wearing an old grey shirt and shabby jeans. He was also wearing a strange hat. He was waving his arms and shouting four-letter words at passers-by. Unbelievable!

Exercise 3

"Twilight" is a dark fantasy novel which was written by Stephenie Meyer. It is the story of Bella Swan, a seventeen-year-old girl whose mother remarries. This is why Bella moves from Phoenix, Arizona, to Forks, Washington, to live with her father. There she meets Edward Cullen, who is an attractive and mysterious boy. He saves her life at the school parking lot when he stops a van that nearly knocks her down. After a while Edward and Bella fall in love. The girl finds out that Edward and his family are vampires who all drink animal blood.
If you want to know how the story continues, you have to read the book. Actually, "The Twilight Saga" is a series which consists of four novels: Twilight, New Moon, Eclipse and Breaking Dawn. If you belong to those people who prefer watching films, there are also five films that you can watch.

Day 3

Exercise 2

1: Scary Island is older than Forever. This is false.
2: Forever won more Oscars than James Blond but fewer than Scary Island. This is false.
3: James Blond is the oldest film. This is true.
4: Forever cost less than Scary Island but more than James Blond. This is false.
5: Scary Island is shorter than James Blond but longer than Forever. This is true.
6: Forever won as many Oscars as Scary Island. This is false.
7: The most expensive film is James Blond. This is true.
8: Scary Island is not as old as James Blond. This is true.
9: Scary Island is not the shortest film. This is true.

Exercise 6

Peter: What's the matter, Megan?
Megan: I'm afraid I won't be able to go to the cinema with you tonight. I have to study for my maths test.
Peter: That's a pity!
Megan: I know. I would love to see "Pepper". Could you tell me tomorrow what it is about?
Peter: I'm sorry. I have never been able to remember the plot of a film.
Megan: Why are you going to the cinema then?
Peter: Because I admire Angelina Jolie. She can do most of her stunts herself.
Megan: That's amazing. A couple of weeks ago her film "Maleficent" was on TV. Unfortunately I couldn't watch it because my little sister was crying all night so I didn't understand a word.
Peter: Never mind. I have it on DVD, so we can watch it at my place whenever you want.
Megan: Great, thanks.

Day 4

Exercise 3

1: If you throw broken dishes at the houses of friends and family on New Year's Eve, they will have good luck in the New Year. This is in Denmark.
2: If you open and close scissors without cutting anything, you will have bad luck. This is in Egypt.
3: If you put your bread upside-down on the table, you will be hungry. This is in France.
4: If you let your wallet or purse hit the floor, you will lose money. This is in Brazil.
5: If you eat 12 grapes one after another when the clock strikes 12 on New Year's Eve, you will have good luck for twelve months. This is in Spain.
6: If you go to sleep with a fan on in your room, it will kill you. This is in South Korea.
7: If bird droppings land on you, you will be rich. This is in Russia.

Exercise 7

Last Friday was a really terrible day. First of all, my alarm clock didn't go off. "I mustn't be late for school!" I shouted and jumped out of bed. When I made breakfast, I dropped an egg on the kitchen floor and after cleaning it up I picked up a cup and accidentally dropped it, smashing it to pieces. Oh no! My mum said, "You don't have to tidy up. I'll do that for you. Run to the bus stop. If you don't hurry, you will miss the bus!"
I had an English test in the third lesson and needed my lucky stone. I was looking for it all over my room but I couldn't find it anywhere. "Come on, hurry up!" I heard my mother shout again. "Mum, I won't pass the test if I don't have my lucky stone!" It was gone!
I grabbed my school bag and rushed to the bus stop only to find out that the bus had already left. Well, I didn't have any time to waste, so I started to run as fast as I could. I looked behind me and saw that a dog was chasing me. How could this day get any worse?
Finally I got to school. I was 20 minutes late and my teacher was angry with me. She said, "If you go to sleep early, you will wake up on time." Thanks, Miss, that's just what I wanted to hear. The English test was more difficult than the last one, I don't think that I passed it. Anyway, there's more to come.
On the way home the bus had a flat tyre and so I had to walk but it started to rain! By the time I was at home I was completely soaked and I had to get changed. After I had put on dry clothes, I realized that I was starving. "All I want now is something to eat", I said to myself. I opened the fridge but it was empty. My sister simply told me, "Some of my classmates were here. I'm sorry. You have to go shopping." What a lousy day!

Day 5

Exercise 5

Last night Matt had an exciting dream. After he had missed the train, he followed it in a hot air balloon and flew on a snow-covered mountain. On top of the mountain Matt put on his skis. After he had gone downhill, he jumped on a ship. He had got off the ship, before he took a motorbike. As fast as he could he went to the station where the train he had missed was waiting. In the morning Matt's mother woke him up and he felt sad because it had only been a dream.

Exercise 7

Dear Agony aunt,
I'm a 13-year-old girl and I'm having a lot of problems at the moment. I don't know who to turn to for help. Six months ago we moved to a new town and my parents started new jobs. They are always very busy and have enough problems themselves. At my new school there are two boys who keep calling me names and the others laugh every time they do it. They also make fun of my clothes and my hairstyle, but they only do it when the teacher isn't around. The other classmates don't seem to like me either. So I never speak to anyone. I feel really depressed and I don't want to go to school anymore. What should I do? Please help me.
Vanessa

Revision 1

Exercise 4

Sally: Hello?
Harry: Hi, Sally, this is Harry. What are you doing?
Sally: I'm watching Harry Potter.
Harry: Were you not watching it when I called you yesterday?
Sally: Yes, that's true. I love Harry Potter. I watch it every day. And what are you doing?
Harry: Nothing. After I had phoned you yesterday, I wanted to rent a Harry Potter DVD but I couldn't get one. Could I come over to your place to watch the film with you?
Sally: Sure, no problem. Bring along some crisps.

Day 6

Exercise 5

Last April we flew to London. First we went to our hotel to check in and get rid of our luggage, then we started our visit with a sightseeing tour. After we had hopped on and off a double decker bus, we got tired and hungry. So we decided to eat fish and chips in a small restaurant where my dad spent a fortune! Next, we visited the London Dungeon which was quite scary. The next day we went to Madame Tussaud's but we had to queue for more than an hour. Afterwards my mother and my sister wanted to go shopping in Oxford Street. We bought some souvenirs, CDs and magazines. When we finally went back to Austria on the third day, we took a ride on the London Eye. London is great!

Day 7

Exercise 2

Here are the answers:
1: Although Los Angeles and San Francisco are much larger, the capital city of California is Sacramento.
2: It's the Pacific Ocean that borders California on the west.
3: The correct answer is Alcatraz. The Statue of Liberty is in New York, the Walk of Fame in Hollywood.
4: Texas is about 60% larger than California.
5: The Brooklyn Bridge is in New York City.
6: 20 million people live in New York (8.4 of them in New York City), 37 million people live in California. So California is right.
7: The Golden State is correct. The Sunshine State is the nickname of Florida, the Empire State is New York.
8: The hottest, driest and the lowest national park is called Death Valley National Park.
9: You will meet Mickey Mouse at Disneyland in Anaheim, but not in Monterey.
10: A lot of film stars, producers and directors live in Beverly Hills.
11: He's actually Austrian – Arnold Schwarzenegger.

Day 8

Exercise 6

Andrea: Peter, what's your favourite band?
Peter: The Thunderbirds.
Andrea: I've never heard of them. Who are they?
Peter: They are four boys from Linz and their band was formed in 2007. Their first concert was played in a small pub in Linz in the same year.
Andrea: Do they sing in German or English?
Peter: At the beginning their lyrics were written in German and their first album was released in German too. But now all their songs are sung in English so that they are understood worldwide.
Andrea: How many albums have been released so far?
Peter: Three. They can only be bought directly from them.

Exercise 8

Interviewer: Welcome Niall, Zayn, Liam, Harry and Louis! Tell me, how were you discovered?
One Direction: We took part in the TV talent show The X Factor. That was in 2010.
Interviewer: When did you release your debut album?
One Direction: Our first album was released in 2011.
Interviewer: How many albums have you released so far?
One Direction: Four, but we're already working on our fifth album.
Interviewer: What about your private lives? Your fans would like to be informed about your partners, your stories …
One Direction: We'd like to keep that to ourselves. Bye!

Day 10

Exercise 7

1: Many people will walk in and out of your life, but only true friends will leave footprints in your hearts.
2: Make new friends but keep the old. One is silver and the other is gold.
3: Some friends come into your life for a reason, others come in for a season.
4: Fake friends are like shadows. They follow you in the sun, but leave you in the dark.
5: Making a million friends is not a miracle. The miracle is to make a friend who will stand up for you when millions are against you.
6: Good friends are like stars. You don't always see them, but you know they are always there.

Irregular Verbs

Infinitive	Past Tense	Past Participle	German
be (am, is, are)	was, were	been	sein
become	became	become	werden
begin	began	begun	beginnen
blow	blew	blown	blasen
break	broke	broken	(zer)brechen
bring	brought	brought	bringen
buy	bought	bought	kaufen
catch	caught	caught	fangen
choose	chose	chosen	auswählen
come	came	come	kommen
cut	cut	cut	schneiden
do	did	done	tun
draw	drew	drawn	zeichnen
drink	drank	drunk	trinken
drive	drove	driven	fahren
eat	ate	eaten	essen
fall	fell	fallen	fallen
feed	fed	fed	füttern
feel	felt	felt	fühlen
fight	fought	fought	kämpfen
find	found	found	finden
fly	flew	flown	fliegen
forget	forgot	forgotten	vergessen
get	got	got	bekommen, werden
give	gave	given	geben
go	went	gone	gehen
grow	grew	grown	wachsen
have	had	had	haben
hear	heard	heard	hören
hide	hid	hidden	verstecken
hit	hit	hit	schlagen
hold	held	held	halten
hurt	hurt	hurt	verletzen
keep	kept	kept	behalten, aufbewahren
know	knew	known	kennen, wissen
leave	left	left	verlassen
let	let	let	lassen
lie	lay	lain	liegen
lose	lost	lost	verlieren
make	made	made	machen
meet	met	met	treffen
pay	paid	paid	bezahlen
put	put	put	setzen, stellen, legen
read	read	read	lesen
ride	rode	ridden	reiten
ring	rang	rung	läuten
run	ran	run	laufen
say	said	said	sagen
see	saw	seen	sehen
sell	sold	sold	verkaufen
send	sent	sent	schicken
set	set	set	untergehen
sing	sang	sung	singen
sit	sat	sat	sitzen
sleep	slept	slept	schlafen
speak	spoke	spoken	sprechen
spend	spent	spent	verbringen, ausgeben
stand	stood	stood	stehen
steal	stole	stolen	stehlen
swim	swam	swum	schwimmen
take	took	taken	nehmen
teach	taught	taught	unterrichten
tell	told	told	erzählen
think	thought	thought	denken
throw	threw	thrown	werfen
understand	understood	understood	verstehen
wake up	woke up	woken up	aufwachen
wear	wore	worn	tragen, anziehen
win	won	won	gewinnen
write	wrote	written	schreiben